WINDOWS 11
SENIORS GUIDE

The Most User-Friendly Seniors and Beginners Manual to Learn Windows 11's Essential Features

Chapter 1: Getting Started Windows 11 ....**6**

Introduction to Windows 11 9

Navigating the Windows 11 Interface 12

    Start Menu Essentials...15

    Taskbar Functions 17

    Managing Multiple Windows and Desktops.........19

Setting Up Your Computer 21

    Connecting to Wi-Fi..23

    Setting Up Printers and Devices 25

Personalizing Windows 11 27

    Customizing the Start Menu 29

    Adjusting the Taskbar 31

    Theme and Background Settings 33

Accessibility Features for Seniors 35

    Magnifier and High Contrast Themes.................38

    Narrator and Speech Recognition 39

    Keyboard Shortcuts & Ease of Access 41

Chapter 2: Internet and Email.................................**43**

Browsing the Web with Edge 46

    Using Tabs and Extensions 48

    Privacy and Security Settings 49

Setting Up and Using Email...50

    Adding Email Accounts.....................................53

    Sending and Receiving Emails...........................55

    Organizing Your Inbox 57

Staying Safe Online 58

    Recognizing and Avoiding Scams 59

    Creating Strong Passwords 61

    Using Antivirus Software 62

Chapter 3: Apps and the Microsoft Store.................**64**

Discovering Useful Apps 66

    Productivity Apps 68

    Social and Communication Apps 69

Installing and Managing Apps.......................................71

    Navigating the Microsoft Store.........................73

    Updating and Uninstalling Apps 74

Entertainment on Windows 11 77

    Streaming Music and Videos 78

    Reading eBooks and News 80

Chapter 4: Files and Folders **82**

  Managing Files and Folders...86

    Creating and Organizing Folders 88

    Copying, Moving, and Deleting Files 90

  Using OneDrive for Cloud Storage 90

    Setting Up OneDrive..92

    Sharing Files and Folders 94

  Protecting Your Data 96

    Backup and Recovery Options..98

    Understanding File History 100

Chapter 5: Security and Maintenance **102**

  Keeping Windows 11 Secure 104

    Windows Security Essentials 106

    Firewalls and Parental Controls 108

  System Maintenance and Updates 110

    Checking for Windows Updates 112

    Optimizing Performance 113

  Troubleshooting Common Issues 114

    Internet Connectivity Problems 116

    Solving Printer and Device Issues 118

Chapter 6: Advanced Features & Customization **120**

  Virtual Desktops and Task View..122

  Using Cortana for Voice Commands 123

    Setting Up Cortana 125

    Practical Uses of Cortana 127

  Tips and Tricks for Power Users..129

    Keyboard Shortcuts 129

Chapter 7: Connecting with Others **131**

  Video Calls and Meetings...133

    Using Skype and Teams 135

    Tips for Better Video Calls 136

  Social Media and Online Communities...138

    Staying Safe on Social Media 140

    Joining Online Communities 141

Chapter 8: Entertainment and Hobbies **143**

  Exploring Windows 11 for Creativity...146

Using Paint 3D and Photos 147

Writing and Blogging Tools 149

Gaming on Windows 11 151

Discovering Games in Microsoft Store 152

Enjoying Games Safely and Responsibly..154

Chapter 9: Health and Well-Being 156

Staying Healthy with Windows 11..157

Health and Fitness Apps 159

Ergonomics and Computer Use...161

Mindfulness and Relaxation..162

Meditation and Mindfulness Apps 164

Customizing for Eye Comfort and Sleep...166

🎁 YOUR EXCLUSIVE BONUS GIFT! 🎁 168

Chapter 1: Getting Started Windows 11

Windows 11 introduces a fresh, streamlined interface designed to enhance productivity and simplify navigation for users of all ages, particularly seniors. At the heart of this new operating system is the Start Menu, relocated to the center of the taskbar for easy access. This change, while subtle, signifies Microsoft's commitment to a more intuitive user experience. The Start Menu itself has been simplified; live tiles have been replaced with a grid of static icons that can be customized, rearranged, and pinned according to personal preference.

Another significant enhancement is the Taskbar, which now features Task View and Widgets. Task View allows users to create and switch between multiple desktops, a boon for organizing different workspaces for personal, work, or hobby-related tasks. Widgets, on the other hand, offer at-a-glance information such as weather, news, and calendar events, directly from the Taskbar. This ensures that important information is readily accessible without cluttering the desktop.

For seniors looking to stay connected with family and friends, Windows 11 has made strides in integrating communication apps directly into the Taskbar. Microsoft Teams is now a staple feature, offering a convenient way to initiate video calls or chats without navigating through multiple apps. This integration underscores Windows 11's focus on connectivity and ease of use.

Navigating the file system has also been refined in Windows 11. The File Explorer has received a facelift, with a more streamlined toolbar replacing the traditional ribbon interface. This change not only simplifies the appearance but also makes common tasks more accessible. Copying, moving, and deleting files can be done with fewer clicks, and the new context-sensitive menu presents options that are relevant to the selected file or folder, reducing clutter and enhancing usability.

In addition to these core features, Windows 11 introduces Snap Layouts and Snap Groups, innovative tools designed to aid in window management. Snap Layouts allow users to easily organize open windows into a predefined layout, optimizing screen real estate and reducing the need to manually resize and position windows. Snap Groups enable users to save and quickly switch between groups of apps that are used together, streamlining workflow and productivity.

These foundational changes in Windows 11 are just the beginning. The operating system is built with flexibility and personalization in mind, offering a range of settings to tailor the user experience to individual needs and preferences. From adjusting the size and color of text for better readability to customizing notification settings to reduce distractions, Windows 11 empowers users to create an environment that suits their unique requirements.

Accessibility is a cornerstone of Windows 11, with features like the Magnifier, High Contrast themes, and Narrator designed to make computing more inclusive for seniors. The Magnifier tool, easily activated with a simple keyboard shortcut (Windows + +), allows users to zoom in on parts of the screen for better visibility. High Contrast themes can be enabled to improve readability by altering color schemes to provide a stark contrast between text and background, making navigation and reading easier on the eyes. The Narrator, a built-in screen reader, offers an auditory interface to interact with the computer, reading aloud text on the screen, which is invaluable for users with limited vision.

Voice typing has also been enhanced in Windows 11, leveraging advanced speech recognition technology to allow for hands-free typing. By pressing Windows + H, users can dictate emails, documents, and even navigate the web, a feature that not only aids those with mobility challenges but also provides a more efficient way to interact with the computer.

For those concerned about privacy and security, Windows 11 introduces state-of-the-art security features to protect against malware, phishing, and other threats. The operating system includes Windows Defender, a robust antivirus program that runs in the background, offering real-time protection without compromising system performance. Additionally, Windows 11 incorporates hardware-based security features like TPM 2.0 and secure boot, ensuring a higher level of protection against sophisticated attacks.

Windows 11 also simplifies the process of staying up-to-date with automatic updates. These updates are designed to be seamless and less intrusive, running in the background and applying outside of active hours to minimize disruptions. This ensures that the system remains secure and performs at its best without requiring manual intervention.

For seniors interested in personalizing their computing experience, Windows 11 offers a myriad of options. The new Settings app is reorganized, making it easier to navigate and find various customization options. Users can change the desktop wallpaper, theme colors, and even the lock screen image to create a more personalized and visually appealing environment. The ease of access settings have been expanded, offering more granular control over visual, auditory, and interaction settings to accommodate a wide range of accessibility needs.

Finally, Windows 11 is designed to be compatible with a wide array of hardware, from traditional desktops and laptops to newer form factors like 2-in-1s and tablets. This compatibility ensures that users can enjoy the latest features and improvements without the need for frequent hardware upgrades, making Windows 11 a practical and accessible choice for seniors looking to stay connected and productive.

Introduction to Windows 11

Windows 11 not only revamps the user interface but also introduces a suite of **accessibility features** designed to accommodate a diverse range of needs and preferences. **Magnifier** functionality is seamlessly integrated, enabling users to enlarge portions of their screen effortlessly with a simple keyboard shortcut, Windows + +. This tool is invaluable for those requiring visual assistance, making text and images more discernible. **High Contrast themes** are another pivotal feature, offering users the ability to switch to color schemes that reduce eye strain and enhance readability. Activating these themes is straightforward, accessible through the ease of access settings, ensuring that anyone can customize their visual experience according to their specific needs.

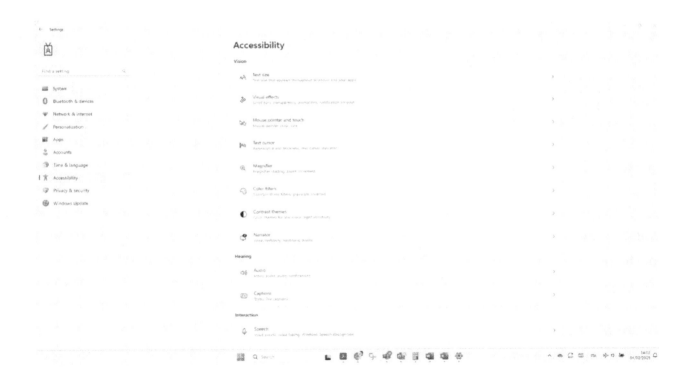

Narrator, Windows 11's built-in screen reader, represents a significant leap forward in making computing accessible to all. By reading aloud text displayed on the screen, the Narrator helps users navigate their computer without having to visually discern icons and text, which is especially beneficial for individuals with limited vision. Engaging the Narrator is as simple as pressing Windows + Ctrl + Enter, demonstrating Microsoft's commitment to accessibility by making these features easily activated.

Voice typing has undergone substantial improvements, leveraging cutting-edge speech recognition technology to facilitate hands-free typing and command input. By pressing Windows + H, users can dictate text effortlessly, a feature that not only benefits those with mobility impairments but also enhances productivity and multitasking capabilities.

Security in Windows 11 has been fortified with advanced measures to safeguard against contemporary cyber threats. **Windows Defender**, the comprehensive antivirus solution, offers real-time protection, scanning for malware, ransomware, and phishing attempts without impeding system performance. Furthermore, Windows 11 incorporates **hardware-based security features** such as TPM 2.0 and secure boot, providing a robust defense against sophisticated attacks. These features underscore the operating system's dedication to user safety, ensuring peace of mind for seniors who may be particularly concerned about online security.

Automatic updates in Windows 11 are designed to be unobtrusive, executing in the background to ensure the system remains updated with the latest security patches and performance improvements. This approach minimizes disruptions, allowing users to maintain productivity and enjoy a seamless computing experience.

Customization options in Windows 11 are extensive, offering users the ability to tailor their computing environment to their liking. The **Settings app** has been reorganized, making it more intuitive to navigate and adjust various system preferences, from changing the **desktop wallpaper** and **theme colors** to customizing the **lock screen**. These personalization features are not merely aesthetic; they also play a crucial role in enhancing usability and comfort, allowing users to configure their workspace in a way that best suits their needs and preferences.

Compatibility with a wide range of hardware ensures that Windows 11 is accessible to as many users as possible, including those who may not have the latest computing equipment. This commitment to inclusivity means that seniors can enjoy the benefits of the latest software innovations without the need for frequent hardware upgrades, aligning with the financial considerations and practical needs of the target audience.

Microsoft's Windows 11 is a testament to the company's dedication to creating an operating system that is not only powerful and secure but also accessible and user-friendly for individuals of all ages and abilities. With its emphasis on simplicity, accessibility, and security, Windows 11 is poised to be a valuable tool for seniors eager to stay connected, productive, and engaged in the digital world.

Navigating the Windows 11 Interface

Windows 11 introduces a **centralized search function** that simplifies finding files, apps, and settings. By clicking on the magnifying glass icon on the Taskbar or pressing Windows + S, users can access a search bar that scans through the computer and the web. This feature is particularly useful for seniors who may not remember the exact location of a file or need quick access to a particular setting without navigating through multiple menus. The search results are intelligently categorized, making it easier to discern between files, applications, images, and web results.

Virtual Desktops offer another layer of organization, allowing users to create separate desktops for different purposes, such as one for personal use and another for work-related activities. This can be accessed by clicking on the Task View icon on the Taskbar or using the shortcut Windows + Tab. From here, users can add or switch between desktops, providing a clutter-free space for each aspect of their digital life. It's a beneficial feature for those who prefer to keep their activities compartmentalized, enhancing focus and efficiency.

The **Action Center** has been redesigned to provide quick access to frequently used settings and notifications. Swiping from the right edge of the screen or clicking on the icon in the lower-right corner of the Taskbar reveals the Action Center panel. Here, seniors can easily toggle connectivity options like Wi-Fi and Bluetooth, adjust brightness and volume, and check new emails or reminders. This consolidation of controls and notifications into a single, accessible location streamlines the user experience, reducing the need to navigate through multiple settings menus.

Widgets have been reintroduced in Windows 11, offering personalized news, weather, calendar, and to-do lists directly from the Taskbar. By clicking on the Widgets icon, users can glance at useful information without opening a browser or specific app. This feature is customizable, allowing users to tailor the content according to their interests and needs, ensuring that relevant information is always at their fingertips.

The **Settings app** itself has been overhauled for better navigation and organization. With a simplified layout and clearer categorization, finding and adjusting various system settings has become more intuitive. Whether it's changing the display resolution, managing privacy settings, or customizing the Taskbar, the Settings app provides a centralized location for all configuration needs. This is particularly advantageous for seniors, as it reduces complexity and enhances the ability to self-manage their computing environment.

For those interested in **personalizing their experience**, Windows 11 offers a wide range of options to adjust the look and feel of the desktop. Right-clicking on the desktop and selecting Personalize opens a menu where users can change their wallpaper, choose a theme, and customize the Start Menu and Taskbar. These personalization options allow seniors to create a computing environment that is both visually pleasing and functionally tailored to their preferences.

In summary, Windows 11 has been designed with a focus on simplicity, accessibility, and personalization. Its interface presents a balanced mix of innovation and familiarity, ensuring that users of all ages, especially seniors, can navigate their computers with ease and confidence. The operating system's thoughtful features and intuitive design principles underscore Microsoft's commitment to making technology accessible to a broader audience, empowering seniors to stay connected and productive in the digital age.

Start Menu Essentials

The Start Menu in Windows 11 serves as the nucleus of your computing experience, offering a streamlined and efficient pathway to your applications, settings, and files. With its central placement on the taskbar, it provides immediate access to everything you need. Understanding how to leverage the Start Menu effectively can significantly enhance your interaction with Windows 11, making it a more intuitive and productive environment.

At its core, the Start Menu is divided into three main sections: the pinned section, the All apps list, and the recommended section. The pinned section allows for quick access to your most frequently used apps. By right-clicking on an app either within the Start Menu or in the All apps list, you can select Pin to Start, which places the app icon in the pinned section for easy access. This customization is crucial for creating a personalized workflow that aligns with your daily needs.

The All apps button, located at the top-right corner of the Start Menu, is your gateway to every application installed on your computer. Clicking on this will display an alphabetical list of apps, making it straightforward to locate and launch any application. For those who prefer keyboard shortcuts, pressing Windows + S and starting to type the application's name is a quick method to search and launch applications without navigating through menus.

The recommended section dynamically displays recently opened files and frequently used apps, learning from your habits to provide quick access to the items you're likely to need next. This feature is particularly beneficial for keeping important documents and applications at your fingertips, streamlining your workflow. However, if you prefer a cleaner Start Menu, this section can be customized or turned off entirely by going into Settings > Personalization > Start and adjusting the options under Show recently opened items in Start, Jump Lists, and File Explorer.

Customizing the Start Menu extends beyond just pinning apps and adjusting the recommended section. Right-clicking on the Start button or pressing Windows + X opens the Quick Link menu, providing access to advanced system tools like the Task Manager, Settings, and the PowerShell. This menu is invaluable for more technical tasks and adjustments, offering a direct line to some of the most powerful features of Windows 11. For those who rely on visual aids, resizing the Start Menu is a simple yet effective way to make it more accessible. Hovering over the edge of the Start Menu until the cursor changes to a double-headed arrow and then clicking and dragging allows you to adjust its size. This flexibility ensures that the Start Menu can be tailored to accommodate various screen sizes and user preferences, enhancing readability and ease of use.

Understanding and customizing the Start Menu in Windows 11 is about more than just aesthetics; it's about optimizing your interaction with your computer to make it as efficient and enjoyable as possible. By taking the time to personalize the Start Menu, you can ensure that your most used applications and files are always within easy reach, making your computing experience more fluid and tailored to your specific needs. Whether it's through pinning your favorite apps, managing the recommended section, or utilizing the Quick Link menu for advanced tasks, the Start Menu is a powerful tool that, when mastered, can significantly enhance your productivity and enjoyment of Windows 11.

Taskbar Functions

The Taskbar in Windows 11 is not just a static tool for navigating or launching applications; it's a dynamic interface that adapts to the needs and habits of its users, especially seniors who appreciate straightforward and efficient interactions with their technology. One of the most notable functions of the Taskbar is its ability to manage and switch between applications with ease. By simply clicking on an application icon, users can bring the application to the forefront, or if the application is not open, launch it directly from the Taskbar. This feature is particularly useful for those who use certain applications frequently, as it eliminates the need to navigate through the Start Menu or search for the application each time.

For applications that are open but not currently in use, the Taskbar provides visual cues to help users keep track of their active tasks. Hovering over an application icon displays a thumbnail preview of the window, allowing users to quickly see the content without needing to switch fully to the application. This can be incredibly helpful when managing multiple documents or websites, as it provides a way to quickly reference information without disrupting the workflow.

Right-clicking on an application icon in the Taskbar opens a jump list, a feature that offers quick access to recent files and common tasks associated with that application. For example, right-clicking on the Microsoft Word icon might show a list of recently edited documents, enabling users to open a file directly without having to launch Word and then navigate through the File menu. This function streamlines the process of accessing frequently used files, making it more efficient and less time-consuming.

The Taskbar also integrates system functions that are essential for maintaining the health and performance of the computer. The notification area, located at the right end of the Taskbar, contains icons for system and application notifications, the network status, the battery level for laptops, and the volume control. Clicking on the date and time displays the calendar and clock, while clicking on the notification icon opens the Action Center, which consolidates notifications and provides quick toggle switches for key settings such as Wi-Fi, Bluetooth, and Focus Assist. This centralization of controls and information makes it easier for users to monitor and adjust their system settings on the fly.

Customization is a key aspect of the Taskbar's functionality, allowing users to tailor its appearance and behavior to their preferences. Users can choose which icons appear in the Taskbar and the notification area, adjust the Taskbar's location on the screen, and even hide the Taskbar when it's not in use. To customize the Taskbar, one would right-click on an empty space on the Taskbar and select Taskbar settings, which opens a menu where various adjustments can be made. For instance, enabling Automatically hide the taskbar in desktop mode can provide a cleaner and more distraction-free environment, particularly beneficial for users who prefer a minimalist desktop.

Moreover, the Taskbar's search function is a powerful tool for finding files, applications, settings, and even web results directly from the desktop. By clicking on the search icon or typing directly when the Taskbar is in focus, users can input their query, and Windows 11 will present relevant results in an organized manner. This feature is invaluable for quickly locating information or applications, especially for users who may not remember the exact location of a file or the name of a setting.

In essence, the Taskbar in Windows 11 is designed to offer a balance of functionality, accessibility, and personalization, ensuring that users, particularly seniors, can navigate their computers with ease and efficiency. Its integration of application management, system monitoring, and quick access functions, combined with the ability to customize its appearance and behavior, makes the Taskbar an indispensable tool in enhancing the user experience on Windows 11.

Managing Multiple Windows and Desktops

The adept management of multiple windows and desktops in Windows 11 is a testament to the operating system's flexibility and user-centric design. This feature is particularly beneficial for users who engage in various tasks simultaneously, allowing for a more organized and efficient computing experience. To further enhance productivity, Windows 11 introduces **Snap Assist**, a tool that significantly simplifies the process of organizing open windows on your screen. By dragging a window to the edge of your screen, Snap Assist automatically suggests a portion of the screen for the window to occupy. This functionality is not only intuitive but also highly customizable, enabling users to create a workspace tailored to their specific needs.

For those who require an even greater level of organization, **Virtual Desktops** offer the capability to segregate work into distinct environments. This is particularly useful for separating personal projects from professional tasks, or for dedicating a desktop to specific applications. Creating a new virtual desktop is as simple as pressing Windows + Tab and selecting the New desktop option at the top of the screen. Switching between desktops can be achieved with the same shortcut, providing a seamless transition that maintains workflow continuity.

Customization plays a pivotal role in the utility of Virtual Desktops. Each desktop can be named and tailored with distinct wallpapers, allowing for immediate visual differentiation. This customization can be accessed by right-clicking on the desired desktop in Task View and selecting Rename or Choose background, making it easier to navigate between tasks and projects.

In addition to these organizational tools, Windows 11 facilitates the management of multiple applications through **Alt + Tab** and **Task View**. The former allows users to quickly switch between open applications, displaying all active windows in a full-screen overlay for easy selection. Task View, on the other hand, offers a comprehensive overview of all open windows and virtual desktops, accessible via Windows + Tab. This feature not only aids in window management but also in the visualization of the entire workspace, enabling users to efficiently allocate their attention and resources.

For those who frequently utilize the same set of applications or documents, **Snap Groups** are a revolutionary feature. By hovering over an application's icon in the Taskbar, users can access a preview of the Snap Group - a collection of apps that were previously snapped together. This allows for the rapid restoration of a working environment, significantly reducing setup time and enhancing productivity.

The integration of these features into Windows 11 underscores Microsoft's commitment to creating an accessible and user-friendly operating system. By leveraging Snap Assist, Virtual Desktops, Snap Groups, and the comprehensive window management tools, users can customize their computing experience to match their unique workflow. This not only maximizes productivity but also ensures that the technology adapts to the user's needs, rather than the other way around. The ability to efficiently manage multiple windows and desktops is not just a feature of Windows 11; it is a fundamental aspect of modern computing that empowers users to perform at their best.

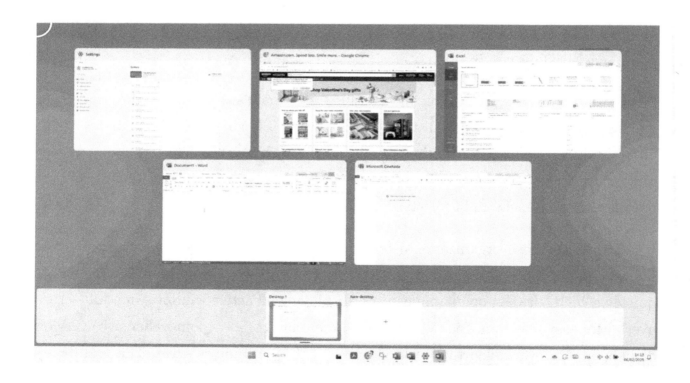

Setting Up Your Computer

To ensure a smooth and efficient setup of your Windows 11 computer, it's crucial to connect to **Wi-Fi** and set up your **printers and devices**. Begin by locating the Wi-Fi icon on the taskbar at the bottom right of your screen. Click on this icon to open a list of available networks. Select your home network, enter the password, and you'll be connected to the internet. This step is essential for downloading updates, browsing the web, and installing new software.

Next, let's focus on connecting printers and other devices. Windows 11 makes this process straightforward. For printers, power on your printer and connect it to your PC either via USB cable or through your local network. Most printers are automatically recognized by Windows 11, which will prompt you to install any necessary drivers. If your printer isn't automatically detected, you can add it manually by going to **Settings > Devices > Printers & scanners > Add a printer or scanner**. Windows will search for and help you complete the installation.

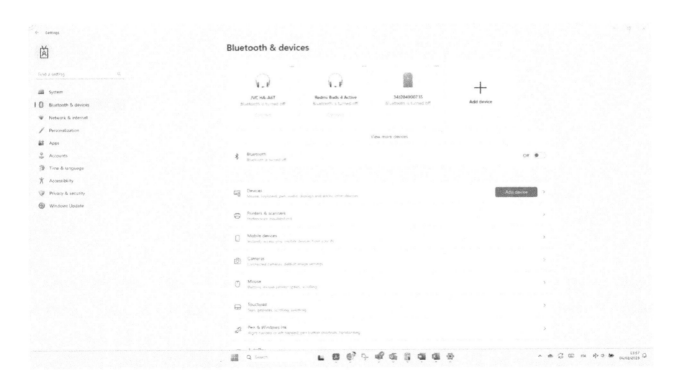

For other peripherals like external hard drives, webcams, or speakers, the process is similarly user-friendly. Simply connect the device to your computer using the appropriate cable, and Windows should recognize it immediately. If drivers are required, Windows will attempt to install them automatically. Should you encounter any issues, the manufacturer's website often provides the latest drivers and installation guides.

Remember, keeping your devices and Windows 11 up to date is crucial for security and performance. Regularly check for updates by navigating to **Settings > Update & Security > Windows Update** and clicking on **Check for updates**. This ensures your computer and connected devices work harmoniously and efficiently, providing you with the best possible experience.

By following these steps, you'll have your computer set up and ready to explore the vast array of features Windows 11 has to offer. Whether you're connecting to the internet, setting up printers, or adding new devices, Windows 11 is designed to make the process as seamless as possible, allowing you to focus on what matters most to you.

Connecting to Wi-Fi

Once you've clicked on the Wi-Fi icon and selected your home network, a prompt will appear asking for your network password. This is the security key you set up with your internet service provider or the one found on your router. After entering the correct password, press `Enter` or click `Connect` to establish your internet connection. It's important to ensure that your password is entered accurately, taking note of any uppercase or lowercase letters, numbers, and special characters, as Wi-Fi passwords are case-sensitive.

If your connection attempt is successful, you'll see a message indicating you are connected to the network, and the Wi-Fi icon will change to show signal strength, a sign that internet access is now available. Should you encounter issues connecting, Windows 11 provides troubleshooting options. You can access these by right-clicking the Wi-Fi icon and selecting `Troubleshoot problems`. This utility can help identify and resolve common connection issues, such as signal strength problems or incorrect network settings.

For those who prefer a continuous connection without the need to log in every time, Windows 11 offers the option to automatically connect to your preferred networks. When entering your password, ensure the `Connect automatically` checkbox is selected. This feature is particularly useful for your home network or any other network you trust and use frequently.

In some cases, you might be in a location with multiple Wi-Fi networks available. Windows 11 makes it easy to manage these connections. By clicking on the Wi-Fi icon, you can view all available networks, their signal strength, and security type. Networks that require a password will display a lock icon. Connecting to a new network follows the same steps as connecting to your home network: select the network, enter the password if required, and click `Connect`.

For enhanced security, especially when connecting to public Wi-Fi networks, consider using a Virtual Private Network (VPN). A VPN encrypts your internet connection, protecting your data from unauthorized access. Windows 11 includes built-in support for VPN connections. To set up a VPN, go to `Settings > Network & Internet > VPN` and click `Add a VPN connection`. Here, you'll enter the details provided by your VPN service, such as the VPN provider, connection name, server name or address, and your login credentials.

Maintaining a stable and secure Wi-Fi connection is crucial for making the most out of Windows 11's features. Whether you're browsing the web, streaming content, or working from home, a reliable internet connection ensures you can stay connected without interruption. By following these steps and recommendations, you can enjoy a seamless online experience with Windows 11, taking full advantage of everything the operating system has to offer.

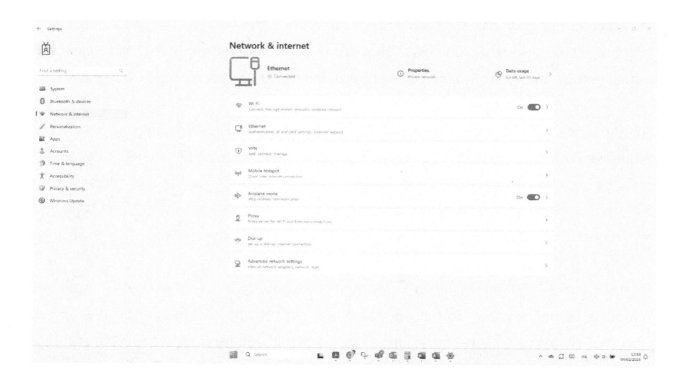

Setting Up Printers and Devices

Once your printer or device is connected and recognized by Windows 11, you might need to delve into the settings to ensure everything is configured correctly for your needs. For printers, this could involve adjusting print quality, setting up duplex printing, or configuring the default paper size. Access these settings by navigating to `Settings > Devices > Printers & scanners`, selecting your printer, and then clicking `Manage`. Here, you'll find a variety of options to customize your printer's functionality to your liking.

For other devices, such as webcams or external hard drives, you may want to adjust settings for optimal performance or to suit your specific requirements. For example, with webcams, you can adjust the video quality or configure privacy settings. To access device settings, right-click on the Start button, select `Device Manager`, and find your device in the list. Right-clicking on the device will provide a menu with options to update drivers, disable the device, or access properties where more detailed settings can be adjusted.

It's also important to regularly check for driver updates to ensure your devices function smoothly with Windows 11. While Windows Update automatically installs important driver updates, you can manually check for updates by going to `Settings > Update & Security > Windows Update` and selecting `View optional updates`. Here, you'll find any available driver updates under the `Driver updates` section. Installing these updates can improve device performance, add new features, and fix any known issues.

For devices that require specific software or applications from the manufacturer, such as graphics tablets or specialized printers, ensure you visit the manufacturer's website to download the latest software version. This software often provides more advanced settings and features than what's available through Windows settings alone.

In cases where a device isn't working as expected, Windows 11 includes troubleshooting tools that can help diagnose and solve common problems. To access these tools, go to `Settings > Update & Security > Troubleshoot`. Here, you can run various troubleshooters for internet connections, playing audio, printers, and more. These troubleshooters can automatically identify and fix issues, making them a valuable resource for resolving device problems quickly.

Remember, the key to efficiently setting up printers and devices on Windows 11 lies in taking the time to explore the settings and options available for each device. By customizing these settings, you can ensure that your devices are optimized for your specific needs and preferences, allowing you to get the most out of your Windows 11 experience. Whether you're printing documents, participating in video calls, or transferring files, taking the time to properly set up and configure your devices will enhance your overall computer usage, making it more enjoyable and productive.

Personalizing Windows 11

Delving deeper into the realm of **personalization** within Windows 11, it becomes evident that the operating system offers a plethora of options to tailor the user experience to one's preferences and needs. Beyond the initial setup of devices and connectivity, personalizing your desktop environment can significantly enhance your interaction with Windows 11, making it more intuitive and enjoyable.

One of the first steps in this customization journey involves **adjusting the desktop background**. Windows 11 provides a variety of stunning images to choose from, or you can select a personal photo that resonates with your aesthetic. To change your desktop background, right-click on the desktop, select Personalize, then click on Background to explore the available options. Whether you prefer a calming landscape, a vibrant abstract piece, or a cherished family photo, the choice is yours.

Following the background, the **theme and color scheme** of Windows 11 can also be adjusted to match your style. The system offers light and dark modes, which not only alter the appearance but can also influence your device's energy consumption. To switch themes, navigate to Settings > Personalization > Colors. Here, you can choose your preferred mode and accent color, which will be reflected across menus, windows, and many applications, providing a cohesive look and feel.

Customizing the **Start Menu** is another powerful way to personalize your Windows 11 experience. By pinning your most-used apps and tools for easy access, you streamline your workflow and save valuable time. To pin an app, simply find it in the Start Menu, right-click, and select Pin to Start. Conversely, if there are pre-pinned apps you don't use, unpinning them can declutter your Start Menu, making it more efficient. This customization extends to the **Taskbar** as well, where you can pin frequently used applications or adjust Taskbar settings for a more streamlined access. To modify Taskbar items, right-click on an empty area of the Taskbar, select Taskbar settings, and then customize it to your liking.

Accessibility features in Windows 11 also play a crucial role in personalization, especially for users with specific needs. Features such as the **Magnifier**, **Narrator**, and **high contrast themes** can be adjusted to improve readability and navigation. These tools are designed to make the computing experience more comfortable and accessible for everyone. To access these features, go to Settings > Accessibility and explore the various options available to tailor your device to your needs.

For those who value efficiency, **keyboard shortcuts** offer a quick way to navigate and manage Windows 11. Customizing these shortcuts can enhance your productivity, allowing you to perform tasks without lifting your hands from the keyboard. While Windows 11 comes with a set of predefined shortcuts, exploring additional combinations and functionalities can unlock new levels of efficiency.

In conclusion, personalizing Windows 11 is not just about aesthetics; it's about creating an environment that aligns with your preferences, enhances your productivity, and makes technology more accessible. By taking the time to explore and adjust these settings, you can transform your computer into a space that feels uniquely yours, proving that with Windows 11, the power to personalize is at your fingertips.

Customizing the Start Menu

The Start Menu in Windows 11 stands as a central hub for accessing your most frequently used applications, settings, and files. Its customization is pivotal for enhancing your computing experience, allowing you to tailor its layout and functionality to suit your individual needs and preferences. By personalizing the Start Menu, you can streamline your workflow, ensuring that the tools and applications you rely on are readily accessible.

To begin customizing the Start Menu, right-click on an empty space within the Start Menu and select Personalize. This action opens the Settings > Personalization > Start menu, where a range of customization options awaits. Here, you can adjust which folders appear on the Start Menu, enabling quick access to your Documents, Downloads, Pictures, and more. For instance, turning on the toggle next to Documents will ensure that a shortcut to your Documents folder is always visible on the Start Menu, providing swift access with a single click.

Another aspect of customization involves managing the apps list. By default, Windows 11 displays a list of all installed applications in the Start Menu. However, you might prefer a cleaner, more streamlined Start Menu. To achieve this, navigate to Settings > Personalization > Start and toggle off the option for Show app list in Start menu. This action hides the full list of apps, allowing you to focus on your pinned items and the dynamic tiles that provide live updates from your applications.

Pinning your favorite apps for easy access is a straightforward process. Simply locate the app you wish to pin in the All Apps list, right-click on it, and select Pin to Start. This places the app's tile on the Start Menu, where you can click and drag it to rearrange its position according to your preference. Grouping related apps together can further enhance your productivity. For example, you might create a group for productivity apps like Word, Excel, and PowerPoint, and another group for communication tools such as Outlook and Teams. To create a group, drag one app tile over another, and Windows 11 will automatically create a group, which you can name for clarity.

Adjusting the size of the Start Menu is another customization that can significantly impact your user experience. If you find the default size too large or too small, simply hover over the top or right edge of the Start Menu until the cursor changes to a resize arrow. Then, click and drag to adjust the Start Menu's size to your liking. This flexibility allows you to accommodate more or fewer apps on the Start Menu, depending on your needs.

Live Tiles offer dynamic content from your apps directly on the Start Menu, such as weather updates, news headlines, or new email notifications. To customize which apps display live updates, right-click on an app tile and select More > Turn live tile on. This enables the app to show real-time information, keeping you informed at a glance. Conversely, if you prefer a static Start Menu without these updates, you can turn off live tiles by following the same steps and selecting Turn live tile off.

In summary, customizing the Start Menu in Windows 11 is a powerful way to personalize your computing environment, making it more responsive to your unique needs and workflow. By taking advantage of these customization options, you can create a Start Menu that not only reflects your personal style but also enhances your productivity and efficiency.

Adjusting the Taskbar

Adjusting the Taskbar in Windows 11 allows for a more personalized and efficient workspace, catering to your unique preferences and workflow requirements. The Taskbar, a long-standing feature of Windows operating systems, has been significantly enhanced in Windows 11, offering users a multitude of customization options to improve accessibility and productivity. By tailoring the Taskbar to your needs, you can ensure that your most frequently used applications, settings, and features are always within easy reach.

To begin customizing the Taskbar, right-click on an empty area of the Taskbar and select `Taskbar settings`. This action will direct you to the Taskbar section of the Windows Settings app, where you can modify various aspects of the Taskbar's appearance and functionality. One of the first adjustments you might consider is the alignment of the Taskbar icons. Windows 11 introduces the ability to center Taskbar icons, which aligns them with the Start button for a more balanced look. However, if you prefer the traditional layout, you can choose to align the icons to the left. This option is found under `Taskbar behaviors` > `Taskbar alignment`, where you can select `Center` or `Left` according to your preference.

Another useful customization is the ability to show or hide specific icons on the Taskbar. For instance, if you frequently use the search function, ensuring the search icon is visible can save time. Conversely, if you rarely use certain features like Task View or Widgets, you can opt to hide these icons to reduce clutter. Navigate to `Taskbar items` and toggle the switches for `Search`, `Task view`, `Widgets`, and `Chat` to show or hide these elements as desired.

For users who prioritize quick access to news, weather, and other updates, the Widgets feature on the Taskbar provides real-time information at a glance. By customizing which widgets appear and how they are displayed, you can stay informed without overwhelming your workspace. Access the Widgets settings directly from the Taskbar by clicking on the Widgets icon and then on the settings icon within the Widgets pane. Here, you can manage your preferences for content types and sources.

Customizing notification area icons is another aspect of Taskbar adjustment that can enhance your computing experience. The notification area, located on the right side of the Taskbar, includes the system tray, which houses icons for system and application notifications. By selecting `Taskbar corner overflow` within the Taskbar settings, you can choose which icons appear directly on the Taskbar and which are hidden in the overflow menu. This allows you to keep essential notifications visible while minimizing distraction from less critical alerts.

For individuals who require easy access to multiple languages or input methods, configuring the Taskbar to display the language bar can be incredibly beneficial. This feature enables quick switching between different keyboard layouts or input languages, a necessity for multilingual users or those who work with multiple languages regularly. To enable the language bar, go to `Time & language` > `Typing` > `Advanced keyboard settings` and select `Use the desktop language bar when it's available`. Once enabled, you can access and adjust language settings directly from the Taskbar.

Personalizing the Taskbar in Windows 11 not only enhances the visual appeal of your desktop but also significantly impacts your efficiency and workflow. By taking the time to explore and adjust the Taskbar settings to suit your preferences, you can create a computing environment that is both functional and enjoyable to use. Whether it's streamlining access to your most-used applications, managing notifications, or optimizing the Taskbar for multilingual use, the customization options available in Windows 11 empower you to tailor your workspace to your specific needs and preferences, ensuring a more productive and satisfying user experience.

Theme and Background Settings

Diving deeper into the personalization of Windows 11, the Theme and Background Settings offer a robust suite of options that allow users to tailor their computing environment to their personal taste and needs. This customization extends beyond mere aesthetics, impacting usability and the overall computing experience. The process of adjusting these settings is straightforward, yet it opens up a plethora of possibilities for personalization.

To change the theme in Windows 11, one would navigate to Settings > Personalization > Themes. Here, Microsoft provides a selection of predefined themes, each comprising a coordinated set of wallpapers, color schemes, and system sounds. For those with a penchant for customization, creating a custom theme is as simple as selecting individual elements like background images, color accents, and sounds to match personal preferences. This feature is particularly beneficial for users who require specific visual settings for better visibility or those who wish to reduce eye strain with darker colors.

Background settings, accessible via Settings > Personalization > Background, allow for further customization. Users can choose a single picture, a slideshow of images, or a solid color as their desktop background. The slideshow option is perfect for users who enjoy a dynamic desktop environment, as it periodically cycles through a selection of photos, keeping the desktop fresh and engaging. For setting up a slideshow, one simply selects a folder containing the desired images, and Windows 11 takes care of the rest, offering controls for shuffle and picture change frequency.

Moreover, the advanced settings provide options to adjust the fit of the background image, accommodating various screen sizes and aspect ratios. Options include fill, fit, stretch, tile, and center, ensuring that any chosen image looks its best on the desktop. These settings are particularly useful for those who use multiple monitors, as they can set different wallpapers for each screen or stretch a single image across all screens for a unified look.

Adjusting the color scheme is another way to personalize the Windows 11 experience. Within Settings > Personalization > Colors, users can select an accent color that highlights various elements of the user interface, such as the Start menu, taskbar, and window borders. Windows 11 offers an automatic option that pulls a dominant color from the current background, or users can manually select a preferred shade. Additionally, there's an option to apply the accent color to the Start menu, taskbar, and action center, further integrating the color scheme throughout the operating system.

For those concerned with readability and eye comfort, Windows 11 includes a high contrast mode, which can be activated via Settings > Ease of Access > High Contrast. This mode increases the color contrast of text, buttons, and other user interface elements, making them more distinguishable and easier on the eyes, especially in low-light conditions or for users with visual impairments.

In summary, the Theme and Background Settings in Windows 11 are designed to cater to a wide range of preferences and needs, allowing users to create a personalized and comfortable computing environment. Whether the goal is to enhance visibility, reduce eye strain, or simply express one's personal style, these settings provide the tools necessary to tailor the desktop experience to individual specifications.

Accessibility Features for Seniors

Windows 11 introduces a suite of **accessibility features** designed with seniors in mind, ensuring that everyone can navigate, understand, and fully utilize their computer, regardless of any physical limitations or preferences for certain types of interfaces. Among the most impactful of these features is the **Magnifier**, a tool that can significantly enhance visibility by zooming into parts of the screen. This is particularly useful for reading small text or examining details in photos. To activate the Magnifier, simply press `Windows` + `+` (plus sign), and to zoom out, `Windows` + `-` (minus sign). The level of zoom can be adjusted to suit individual needs, making digital content more accessible than ever before.

Another critical aspect of Windows 11's accessibility offerings is the **High Contrast Themes**. These themes are designed to increase readability by altering the color scheme to present a higher contrast between the background and the text or icons on the screen. This feature can be activated by navigating to `Settings > Ease of Access > High Contrast`. Here, users can choose from a variety of pre-set themes or customize their own, adjusting the color of text, hyperlinks, buttons, and background to create a personalized computing experience that is easier on the eyes.

The **Narrator** is a screen-reading app that reads aloud text on the screen, including text within images, providing an invaluable resource for those with significant vision impairments or those who prefer auditory learning. It can be turned on by pressing `Ctrl` + `Windows` + `Enter`. The Narrator settings allow users to customize voice settings, speed, and pitch to match personal listening preferences, making it easier to interact with your PC without relying on visual cues.

Speech Recognition in Windows 11 empowers users to control their computer using voice commands, from opening applications to dictating and editing documents, or even navigating the web. This feature can be set up by going to `Settings > Time & Language > Speech`, enabling hands-free operation of the computer, which can be particularly beneficial for individuals with mobility challenges.

These features underscore Windows 11's commitment to creating an inclusive environment where technology is accessible to everyone. By leveraging these tools, seniors can enjoy a more comfortable and productive computing experience, tailored to their unique needs and preferences.

Building on the foundation of inclusivity, **Keyboard Shortcuts** offer a streamlined way to navigate Windows 11, reducing the reliance on a mouse or touchpad, which can be cumbersome for some users. For instance, pressing `Windows` + `D` instantly minimizes all open windows to show the desktop, while `Alt` + `Tab` allows users to switch between open applications quickly. These shortcuts can significantly enhance productivity and ease of use, making them a valuable tool for seniors aiming to optimize their computing experience.

The **Ease of Access Center**, found under `Settings > Ease of Access`, serves as a central hub for all accessibility settings, providing quick access to features like the Magnifier, Narrator, High Contrast Themes, and more. It also includes options for **Closed Captions**, **Mouse Pointer** adjustments, and **Keyboard** settings, allowing users to customize their experience to suit their needs. For example, the mouse pointer can be made larger and changed to a more visible color, while keyboard settings can be adjusted to enable sticky keys, which is beneficial for those who have difficulty pressing multiple keys at once.

Moreover, **Windows 11** introduces **Voice Typing**, enhancing the Speech Recognition capabilities. This tool, activated by pressing `Windows` + `H`, allows users to dictate text effortlessly, offering real-time transcription that can be particularly useful for composing emails, documents, or browsing the internet. Voice Typing is designed to understand natural speech patterns, making it a powerful feature for seniors who may find typing challenging or prefer speaking over typing.

In addition to these built-in features, Windows 11 supports a range of **third-party accessibility applications** that can be downloaded from the Microsoft Store, offering even more customization and support options. From screen readers to magnification apps, the ecosystem of tools available can cater to a wide array of needs, ensuring that every user can find the solutions that best fit their accessibility requirements.

By embracing these accessibility features, seniors can navigate Windows 11 with confidence and comfort, making the most of their computer's capabilities. Whether it's through voice commands, high-contrast visuals, or keyboard shortcuts, Windows 11 is equipped to provide a user-friendly experience that respects the diversity of its user base. These tools not only empower seniors to maintain their independence but also enrich their interaction with technology, opening up new avenues for exploration, learning, and connection in the digital age.

Magnifier and High Contrast Themes

The Magnifier tool in Windows 11 is a powerful aid for enhancing visibility, allowing users to zoom into specific areas of their screen with ease. To activate the Magnifier, one simply needs to press Windows + + (plus sign). This action zooms in on the screen, making text, icons, and other details more visible and easier to interact with. For those who need to adjust the level of magnification, continuing to press Windows + + will increase the zoom, while pressing Windows + - (minus sign) will decrease it, offering a range of magnification levels to accommodate various visual needs. The Magnifier settings also provide options for different modes of magnification, such as full screen, lens, or docked, allowing users to choose the most suitable option for their specific tasks. For instance, the lens mode acts like a magnifying glass that follows the cursor, providing a focused area of magnification, which can be particularly useful for reading or detailed work.

High Contrast Themes are another essential feature for improving readability and reducing eye strain. These themes alter the color scheme of the user interface to create a higher contrast between background and text, making it easier for those with visual impairments or preferences for certain color combinations to use their computer. To enable High Contrast Themes, navigate to Settings > Ease of Access > High Contrast. Here, users can select from a variety of pre-set high contrast themes or customize their own by choosing specific colors for text, hyperlinks, buttons, and background. This level of customization ensures that users can create a visual environment that meets their individual needs, enhancing their overall computing experience.

Both the Magnifier and High Contrast Themes are integral to Windows 11's suite of accessibility features, designed to make the operating system more inclusive and user-friendly. These tools not only facilitate ease of use for individuals with visual impairments but also offer options for personalizing the visual aspects of the computer to suit each user's preferences and requirements. By adjusting these settings, seniors can enjoy a more comfortable and accessible computing environment, enabling them to engage with technology more effectively and with greater confidence.

Moreover, the integration of these features within the Ease of Access Center underscores Microsoft's commitment to accessibility, providing a centralized location for adjusting various settings to improve the user experience. This approach allows for a more intuitive and streamlined process for customizing accessibility options, ensuring that users can easily find and adjust the settings they need without navigating through multiple menus. The emphasis on accessibility and customization within Windows 11 demonstrates a thoughtful consideration of diverse user needs, making technology more accessible and enjoyable for everyone, regardless of their age or abilities.

Narrator and Speech Recognition

The Narrator in Windows 11 is an advanced screen-reading tool that transforms the text on your screen into speech, allowing users with vision impairments or those who prefer auditory learning to navigate their computer more effectively. To activate the Narrator, users can press `Ctrl` + `Windows` + `Enter`, a shortcut that instantly turns on this feature, making the digital content on the screen accessible through audio. The customization options within the Narrator settings are extensive, enabling users to adjust the voice, speed, and pitch. This flexibility ensures that the auditory output meets the user's preferences, making the experience as comfortable and beneficial as possible. For instance, adjusting the speech speed is crucial for users who may need more time to comprehend the spoken content, whereas others might prefer a faster pace for efficiency. The Narrator also offers a feature called "Scan Mode," which can be toggled on or off by pressing `Caps Lock` + `Space`. This mode allows users to navigate through apps, email, and webpages using just their keyboard, highlighting the importance of keyboard navigation for accessibility.

Speech Recognition in Windows 11 stands as a testament to the operating system's commitment to inclusivity, providing users the ability to control their computer and dictate text using voice commands. This feature is particularly empowering for individuals with mobility impairments or those who find typing to be a challenge. To set up Speech Recognition, navigate to `Settings` > `Time & Language` > `Speech`, where you can initiate the voice recognition feature. Once activated, it allows for a wide range of voice commands, from opening applications to dictating and editing documents or browsing the internet. The system is designed to understand natural speech patterns, which means users can interact with their computer in a more intuitive and natural way. For example, saying "Start Narrator" or "Open Microsoft Edge" can perform tasks without the need for physical interaction, showcasing the seamless integration of voice commands into the computing experience.

Both Narrator and Speech Recognition embody the strides Microsoft has made in making Windows 11 not just more accessible, but also more intuitive for a diverse range of users. The emphasis on customization and flexibility within these features ensures that users can tailor their computing environment to their specific needs and preferences. For seniors, this means the ability to maintain independence and productivity in their digital interactions, whether it's staying connected with loved ones, managing personal finances, or pursuing hobbies online. The integration of these advanced accessibility features within Windows 11 highlights an ongoing commitment to breaking down barriers and creating a more inclusive digital world. By leveraging the power of technology, seniors are not only able to navigate their computers with ease but also embrace the vast possibilities that come with being connected in the digital age. The tools provided within Windows 11, such as Narrator and Speech Recognition, are more than just features; they are gateways to empowerment, enabling users to interact with technology on their terms and according to their unique needs.

Keyboard Shortcuts & Ease of Access

The **Ease of Access Center** in Windows 11 stands as a testament to Microsoft's commitment to inclusivity, providing a centralized hub for all accessibility settings. This comprehensive suite of tools is designed to cater to a wide range of needs, ensuring that every user can customize their computing experience for maximum comfort and efficiency. For seniors, navigating through these options can significantly enhance their interaction with technology, making digital spaces more navigable and less intimidating.

One of the most practical features within the Ease of Access Center is the ability to adjust **Mouse Pointer** visibility. By navigating to `Settings > Ease of Access > Cursor & Pointer`, users can choose from a variety of sizes and colors for their mouse pointer, making it easier to follow on the screen. This adjustment is particularly beneficial for those with visual impairments or anyone who finds the default pointer too small or not contrasted enough against their background.

Similarly, the **Text Cursor** customization options, found under `Settings > Ease of Access > Text Cursor`, allow users to increase the size and change the color of the text cursor, thereby improving visibility and reducing strain during text entry tasks. This feature is a boon for composing emails, writing documents, or engaging in any activity that involves a significant amount of typing.

For individuals who find navigating via a keyboard more intuitive or physically easier than using a mouse, **Keyboard Shortcuts** are indispensable. Windows 11 supports a vast array of shortcuts designed to streamline navigation and simplify common tasks. For example, `Ctrl + C` for copying selected text or files and `Ctrl + V` for pasting them elsewhere are universally recognized shortcuts that can save time and reduce the physical effort of navigating menus. Moreover, `Alt + Tab` allows users to switch quickly between open applications, and `Windows + L` locks the computer, providing a quick way to secure the system when stepping away.

In addition to these general shortcuts, Windows 11 introduces new key combinations that leverage its unique features. `Windows + A` opens the Action Center, providing quick access to notifications and settings such as Wi-Fi, Bluetooth, and brightness. `Windows + S` activates the search bar, enabling users to find applications, files, and settings or perform web searches directly from the desktop. These shortcuts, among others, are not just conveniences; they represent critical pathways for seniors to maintain independence and confidence in using their computers.

The **Narrator** feature, a cornerstone of Windows 11's accessibility offerings, offers an enhanced experience with customizable voice options. Activated by `Ctrl + Windows + Enter`, the Narrator reads aloud text on the screen, including buttons and notifications, making it invaluable for users with significant vision impairments. Within the Narrator settings, users can adjust the speed, pitch, and volume of the voice to suit their preferences, as well as select from a range of voices for a more personalized experience.

Furthermore, **Magnifier** functionality is easily toggled on and off with `Windows + Plus` to zoom in and `Windows + Minus` to zoom out, providing on-the-fly visual assistance. This tool can be configured to operate in full screen, lens, or docked mode, offering flexibility in how content is magnified to meet the user's specific needs.

The integration of these features within the Ease of Access Center, accessible via `Settings > Ease of Access`, underscores the importance of accessibility in Windows 11. By centralizing these settings, Microsoft ensures that users can effortlessly customize their experience without navigating through multiple menus or remembering complex pathways. This approach not only simplifies the process of making adjustments but also empowers users to explore and utilize the full range of accessibility features available, fostering a sense of autonomy and competence.

Chapter 2: Internet and Email

Browsing the web with Microsoft Edge offers a gateway to the world's information, entertainment, and social platforms. Microsoft Edge, the default browser in Windows 11, is designed with both speed and security in mind, ensuring that seniors can safely explore the internet. To start, one simply clicks on the Edge icon on the taskbar or searches for it in the Start menu. Upon launching Edge, users are greeted with a customizable homepage that includes a search bar, frequently visited sites, and news tailored to their interests.

For those unfamiliar with web browsers, the address bar at the top of the Edge window is where you type website addresses (URLs) directly or enter search terms. Microsoft Edge uses Bing as its default search engine, but users can change this to Google, Yahoo, or another preferred search engine through the settings menu by navigating to Settings > Privacy, search, and services > Address bar and search. This flexibility allows users to tailor their browsing experience to their preferences.

Navigating websites is straightforward with the back and forward buttons located near the top-left corner of the browser window, enabling users to move through their browsing history easily. The refresh button, symbolized by a circular arrow, reloads the current page, useful for updating content or correcting loading issues.

Bookmarks are a powerful feature for keeping track of favorite websites. In Edge, these are called "Favorites," and adding a page to Favorites is as simple as clicking the star icon in the address bar and choosing where to save it. Managing Favorites is done through the Favorites menu, where users can organize their saved sites into folders, making them easy to find later.

Tabs are another key feature, allowing users to have multiple web pages open at the same time within a single browser window. To open a new tab, one clicks the + icon next to the last tab or uses the keyboard shortcut Ctrl + T. Closing a tab is just as easy, with a click on the X on the tab or by pressing Ctrl + W. For those who accidentally close a tab, pressing Ctrl + Shift + T will reopen it, a handy trick that can save time and frustration.

Privacy and security settings in Edge are designed to protect users from malicious websites and tracking by advertisers. The browser offers several levels of tracking prevention, ranging from basic to strict, which can be adjusted in Settings > Privacy, search, and services. Additionally, Edge provides an InPrivate browsing mode, which can be accessed by clicking on the menu button (three dots) in the top-right corner and selecting New InPrivate window. InPrivate browsing does not save browsing history, cookies, or temporary files, offering an extra layer of privacy when needed.

For those looking to personalize their browsing experience further, Microsoft Edge supports extensions, small software programs that add new features or functionality to the browser. Extensions range from ad blockers and password managers to note-taking tools and social media enhancements. To explore available extensions, users can visit the Microsoft Edge Add-ons store, accessible through Edge menu > Extensions > Get extensions for Microsoft Edge. Installing an extension is straightforward, and each comes with its settings for customization and control.

In the next part, we will delve deeper into using tabs and extensions effectively, enhancing the browsing experience, and ensuring online privacy and security through tailored settings and practices.

Delving into the utilization of **tabs** and **extensions** can significantly enhance the browsing experience on Microsoft Edge. Tabs allow for a more organized and efficient way to manage multiple web pages without cluttering the desktop with numerous browser windows. For instance, when researching a topic, users can open each reference site in a new tab, enabling quick comparison and reference back without losing their place. This method is particularly useful for seniors who are working on projects, planning trips, or simply exploring their interests online. The ability to **right-click** on a tab and select

"Pin" ensures that frequently visited sites like email or news pages remain easily accessible at the start of the tab row, reducing the effort needed to navigate to these sites.

Extensions further tailor the browsing experience to the user's needs. For example, an ad blocker can make browsing more pleasant by removing intrusive advertisements, while a password manager helps in securely storing and autofilling login information, simplifying access to online accounts. It's important to exercise caution when installing extensions, ensuring they are sourced from reputable developers to avoid compromising security. A good practice is to read reviews and check the number of downloads before adding an extension to Edge, ensuring it's widely trusted.

Privacy and security are paramount, especially for seniors who may be more vulnerable to online scams and phishing attempts. Edge's **tracking prevention** feature is instrumental in blocking trackers from websites that the user hasn't visited, providing a balance between privacy and a personalized web experience. For enhanced security, it's advisable to set the tracking prevention to **"Strict"** mode, which blocks a majority of trackers across all sites. However, this setting might cause some sites to not function correctly, in which case, users can adjust permissions for specific websites by clicking the **lock icon** in the address bar.

InPrivate browsing mode is a valuable tool for those who wish to keep their online activities private, particularly when using shared or public computers. By ensuring that browsing history, cookies, and temporary files are not saved, InPrivate mode offers an additional layer of privacy, making it ideal for activities like online banking or shopping.

For seniors looking to stay informed and secure online, understanding and configuring **privacy and security settings** in Edge is crucial. Navigating to Settings > Privacy, search, and services allows users to review and adjust these settings, including managing permissions for cookies, location access, and camera and microphone use. Regularly reviewing these settings ensures that users maintain control over their personal information and browsing data.

In conclusion, mastering the use of tabs and extensions, along with a thorough understanding of privacy and security settings, empowers seniors to navigate the web with confidence and ease. By leveraging these features, users can create a browsing environment that is not only efficient and organized but also secure and tailored to their personal preferences. This approach to internet browsing not only enhances the user experience but also reinforces the importance of online safety and privacy, ensuring a more enjoyable and secure digital life.

Browsing the Web with Edge

Microsoft Edge, the default web browser on Windows 11, offers a seamless and secure browsing experience tailored for users of all ages, including seniors. With its intuitive interface and a host of features designed to enhance privacy, accessibility, and ease of use, Edge stands out as a reliable choice for navigating the internet.

Privacy and Security Settings in Edge are paramount, providing users with control over their online footprint. To access these settings, click on the three dots (...) at the top right corner of the browser, select Settings, and then navigate to Privacy, search, and services. Here, you can adjust the tracking prevention to your preferred level (Basic, Balanced, or Strict), which determines how third-party trackers are handled. Additionally, the **Clear browsing data** option allows you to delete your browsing history, cookies, and cached files, ensuring your personal information remains private.

Using Tabs and Extensions significantly enhances the browsing experience. To open a new tab, simply click on the + icon next to the existing tab. This feature is particularly useful for keeping related web pages organized under one window. Extensions, on the other hand, add functionality to Edge. They can be accessed and installed by clicking on the three dots (...), selecting Extensions, and then exploring the Microsoft Edge Add-ons store. Whether it's ad blockers, password managers, or reading aids, extensions can tailor the browser to suit your specific needs.

Favorites and Bookmarks are essential for quick access to frequently visited websites. To bookmark a page, click on the star icon (☆) in the address bar and choose Add to favorites. You can organize these bookmarks into folders for easy retrieval, making it a breeze to find your preferred news sites, email services, or hobby-related pages.

Reading View is another standout feature for seniors, stripping away distractions and presenting web articles in a clean, easy-to-read format. Activate it by clicking on the book icon (📖) in the address bar when it appears. This mode not only simplifies the page layout but also allows for text size adjustments and background color changes, catering to various reading preferences and reducing eye strain.

For those who prefer voice commands, **Using Cortana with Microsoft Edge** offers a hands-free browsing experience. Activate Cortana by clicking on the microphone icon in the search bar and speak your query. From setting reminders to looking up information, integrating Cortana enhances the functionality of Edge, making it more accessible for users who may find typing or navigation challenging.

In conclusion, Microsoft Edge embodies a user-friendly approach to web browsing, emphasizing privacy, customization, and accessibility. Its features are designed to accommodate the needs and preferences of senior users, ensuring a comfortable and productive online experience. By leveraging these tools, seniors can navigate the web confidently, staying connected and informed in the digital age.

Using Tabs and Extensions

Extensions in Microsoft Edge can significantly enhance your browsing experience by adding new functionalities that are not available by default. For instance, if you often find yourself struggling to remember passwords, a password manager extension could be invaluable. These tools store your passwords in a secure vault and automatically fill them in when you visit websites, ensuring that you can maintain strong, unique passwords for each of your accounts without having to remember them all. To install a password manager, navigate to the Microsoft Edge Add-ons store by clicking on the three dots (...) in the upper right corner of the browser, selecting Extensions, and then searching for "password manager". Once you find an extension you trust, click Get to install it. After installation, you might need to create an account with the service (if you don't already have one) and then follow the instructions to add your passwords to the vault.

For those interested in enhancing their privacy online, ad blockers are another popular category of extensions. Ad blockers work by preventing advertisements from loading on web pages, which can speed up your browsing and protect you from potentially malicious ads. To add an ad blocker, follow the same steps as you would for any other extension: access the Microsoft Edge Add-ons store, search for "ad blocker", and choose one with good reviews and a high number of users. After installing, most ad blockers will begin working immediately, though some may offer customization options to block or allow ads on specific websites.

Reading enthusiasts might appreciate extensions designed to improve the reading experience on the web. These can range from tools that adjust the font size and background color of web pages for easier reading to extensions that remove clutter and distractions, leaving only the main content of an article. To find reading aids, search the Microsoft Edge Add-ons store for terms like "reading view" or "readability". Once installed, these extensions often add a button to the browser's toolbar that you can click whenever you're on a page you'd like to read. Some will automatically detect articles and offer the improved reading view without any input needed.

It's important to note that while extensions can greatly enhance your browsing experience, they should be used judiciously. Each extension you install can impact the performance of your browser, and, more critically, extensions have access to your browsing data, which can pose privacy concerns. Always read reviews and research the developer before installing an extension, and regularly review and remove any extensions you no longer use.

By thoughtfully selecting and managing extensions, you can tailor Microsoft Edge to better meet your needs, making your online experience more productive, secure, and enjoyable. Whether it's managing passwords more efficiently, blocking unwanted ads, or making web pages easier to read, there's likely an extension that can help. Remember to approach each new extension with a critical eye, ensuring it comes from a reputable source and offers clear benefits without compromising your privacy or browser performance.

Privacy and Security Settings

The Privacy, search, and services section within Microsoft Edge's settings is a cornerstone for safeguarding your digital footprint, but it extends beyond tracking prevention and clearing browsing data. Delving deeper, the Cookies and site permissions settings play a crucial role in managing how websites interact with your browser. Here, you can fine-tune permissions for sites to access your location, camera, microphone, and notifications. This granular control ensures that only trusted websites have access to certain functionalities, enhancing your online security.

For seniors concerned about inadvertently downloading malicious software, Edge offers an additional layer of protection through the Microsoft Defender SmartScreen. This feature automatically assesses the safety of websites you visit and files you download, blocking anything deemed unsafe. To ensure this feature is active, navigate to Settings > Privacy, search, and services and verify that Microsoft Defender SmartScreen is turned on. This proactive measure significantly reduces the risk of encountering phishing attacks or malware, providing peace of mind while browsing.

Another noteworthy feature is the Payment info setting under Profiles. While convenient for those who frequently shop online, storing payment information in your browser can pose a risk if not managed properly. If you choose to use this feature, regularly review and remove outdated or unnecessary payment methods to minimize exposure. Additionally, leveraging Edge's ability to sync across devices can be a double-edged sword. Syncing favorites, passwords, and payment information across devices offers unparalleled convenience, but it's vital to secure all devices with strong, unique passwords and consider using multi-factor authentication where available to prevent unauthorized access.

The Address bar and search settings further exemplify Edge's commitment to user privacy and control. Here, you can customize your search engine preferences and decide whether search suggestions appear as you type. While these suggestions can speed up your browsing experience, they also involve sending your typed text to your search engine. If privacy is a paramount concern, you may opt to disable this feature, trading off convenience for increased privacy.

Lastly, the Family safety feature is a testament to Edge's versatility in providing a safe browsing environment for all ages. By setting up family accounts, seniors can ensure a safer online experience for grandchildren or other young family members when they use the device. This feature allows for content filtering, screen time management, and activity monitoring, all customizable to fit the needs of each family member.

In navigating these settings, it's evident that Microsoft Edge empowers users with comprehensive tools to manage their online privacy and security. By familiarizing yourself with these options and regularly reviewing your settings, you can tailor your browsing experience to align with your privacy preferences and security needs. Remember, the digital world is ever-evolving, and staying informed about these features is key to safeguarding your online presence.

Setting Up and Using Email

To **set up an email account** in Windows 11, you'll primarily use the **Mail** app, a pre-installed application that simplifies the process of managing your email communications. The first step involves launching the Mail app from the Start menu. Upon opening the app for the first time, you may be prompted to add an account. Select **Add account** to begin the setup process. Windows 11 supports various email services, including Outlook.com, Google, Yahoo, and others. Choose your email provider from the list. If your provider is not listed, select **Other account** to manually input server details.

For most major email services, you will only need to enter your **email address** and **password**. The Mail app automatically configures server settings in the background, making this process as seamless as possible. However, if you select **Other account**, you may need to know your **IMAP**, **SMTP**, and **SSL** requirements. These settings are typically available on your email provider's support website.

After entering your credentials, click **Sign in**. The Mail app will then sync your email, which might take a few minutes depending on the size of your inbox. Once synced, your email account is ready to use. You can add multiple accounts by repeating these steps, allowing you to manage all your emails in one place.

Sending an email is straightforward. In the Mail app, click **New mail**. A new window opens where you can enter the recipient's email address, subject, and the body of your message. If you wish to add attachments, click the **Attach** icon, usually represented by a paperclip, and select the files you want to include. After composing your email, click **Send**.

Organizing your inbox can greatly enhance your email experience. The Mail app offers several tools for this purpose. You can create folders to categorize your emails. Right-click on your account name and select **New folder**. Give your folder a name that reflects its contents, such as "Family" or "Bills". To move emails into a folder, simply drag and drop them into the desired folder or right-click an email, select **Move to**, and choose the folder.

Customizing settings can make your email experience more personalized. Click the **Settings** gear icon in the bottom left corner of the Mail app, then select **Manage accounts**. Choose an account to adjust settings like **sync options**, **email signature**, and **notification preferences**. Tailoring these settings can help streamline your workflow and ensure you're notified of important emails in a manner that suits your lifestyle.

Remember, the **Search** function in the Mail app is a powerful tool for finding specific emails. You can search by sender, subject, or a keyword within the email body. This feature is particularly useful as your inbox grows.

By following these steps, you can effectively manage your email in Windows 11, staying connected with friends, family, and colleagues. The Mail app's integration with Windows 11 makes it a convenient and user-friendly choice for your email needs.

Adding Email Accounts

Once you have successfully set up your initial email account using the Mail app in Windows 11, adding additional email accounts follows a similar straightforward process, enabling you to consolidate all your email communications in one convenient location. Whether you're managing personal, professional, or a mix of email accounts, the Mail app accommodates a diverse range of email services, including but not limited to Outlook.com, Google Mail (Gmail), Yahoo Mail, and many others that support IMAP or POP protocols.

To add another email account, open the Mail app and navigate to the Accounts section found on the left sidebar. Here, you will see a list of your currently added accounts and an option to Add account. Clicking on this will prompt you with the same setup process as before. Select your email provider from the presented list or choose Advanced setup if your provider is not listed or you need to enter specific server settings manually.

For users opting for Advanced setup, you will be required to know your email account's IMAP or POP and SMTP server settings. These settings are crucial for receiving and sending emails, respectively, and can usually be found on your email provider's help or support pages. For IMAP accounts, you will typically enter something akin to imap.provider.com for the incoming mail server and smtp.provider.com for the outgoing mail server, replacing provider.com with your email provider's domain. Additionally, ensure that the correct ports are used (often 993 for IMAP with SSL encryption and 587 for SMTP with TLS encryption) and that SSL encryption is enabled for both incoming and outgoing servers to secure your email communications.

After entering your additional email account details, click Sign in. The Mail app will then verify your credentials and, upon successful authentication, add the account to your list. The app will begin syncing your emails, which, depending on the size of your inbox and the speed of your internet connection, might take some time. Once the sync is complete, you can access the newly added email account from the Accounts section on the left sidebar of the Mail app.

Managing multiple email accounts in the Mail app allows you to seamlessly switch between inboxes and folders, making it easier to keep track of your communications without the need to log in and out of different webmail interfaces. You can customize the settings for each account, such as sync frequency, notification preferences, and signature, by selecting the account from the Accounts list and choosing Account settings.

For those who prefer a unified view, the Mail app offers a combined inbox feature, where emails from all your added accounts can be viewed together, streamlining the process of checking your emails. However, if you prefer to keep your emails separate, you can easily toggle between accounts using the sidebar.

Remember, while the Mail app provides a convenient way to manage your email accounts, it's important to regularly review the security settings of each account, especially if you're using public or shared computers. Ensure that your passwords are strong and unique for each account, and consider enabling two-factor authentication for an added layer of security on your email accounts where available.

By following these steps, you can efficiently manage multiple email accounts in Windows 11, keeping your digital communications organized and accessible in one place. Whether you're staying in touch with family and friends, managing your professional correspondence, or keeping up with your subscriptions and online accounts, the Mail app's flexibility and user-friendly interface make it an invaluable tool for email management.

Sending and Receiving Emails

Upon mastering the addition of email accounts and navigating the Mail app's interface, the next critical step involves the proficient handling of **sending and receiving emails**, a fundamental aspect of digital communication. The Mail app in Windows 11 is designed to streamline this process, ensuring that even those new to email can execute these tasks with ease and confidence.

When preparing to **send an email**, one begins by clicking on the New mail button, which unveils a composition window. Here, the **To** field is where you input the recipient's email address. If sending to multiple recipients, separate each address with a semicolon. The **Cc** (Carbon Copy) and **Bcc** (Blind Carbon Copy) fields serve to include others in the email conversation either transparently or privately, respectively. The **Subject** line should succinctly summarize the email's purpose, providing a clear indication of its content at a glance.

Crafting the body of the email allows for a range of formatting options, from basic text to the inclusion of hyperlinks, bullet points, and numbered lists, enhancing the clarity and visual appeal of your message. The Mail app also supports the attachment of files—be it documents, images, or other media—by clicking the **Attach** icon. This functionality is crucial for sharing documents or photos with colleagues, friends, and family. When the email composition satisfies your intent, pressing the **Send** button dispatches the message to the recipient's inbox, a process typically completed within moments.

Receiving emails is an equally straightforward affair. The Mail app automatically checks for new messages at regular intervals, a frequency that can be adjusted in the account settings. Upon receiving new emails, they appear in the inbox, where clicking on an email subject opens it for reading. The app provides options to **Reply**, **Reply All**, or **Forward** the email, facilitating ongoing communication and the sharing of information with others. For emails that require a future response or action, the **Flag** feature serves as a useful reminder, marking the email for easy identification.

For those managing a high volume of emails, the Mail app's **search functionality** proves invaluable. By entering keywords, sender names, or dates into the search bar, users can quickly locate specific emails among the multitude in their inbox. This tool is especially beneficial for retrieving important messages or attachments without the need to manually sift through extensive email histories.

Moreover, the **Junk Email** folder warrants attention, as it filters out potential spam or phishing attempts. However, it's prudent to periodically review this folder to ensure legitimate emails haven't been mistakenly categorized as junk. If such an error is found, marking the email as **Not Junk** will move it back to the inbox and help refine the filtering algorithm.

The integration of **email rules** is a feature for those looking to automate the organization of their inbox. By setting criteria based on sender, subject, or keywords, emails can be automatically moved to designated folders, marked as read, or flagged. This level of customization aids in maintaining an organized and efficient email environment, particularly beneficial for users managing a high volume of correspondence.

In leveraging these capabilities within the Mail app, users are equipped to manage their email communications effectively. The app's design, emphasizing simplicity and functionality, ensures that users can remain connected and productive, fulfilling the essential need to communicate in today's digital age. The Mail app, with its intuitive interface and comprehensive feature set, stands as a testament to Windows 11's commitment to accessibility and user-friendliness, catering to the needs of a diverse user base, including the senior demographic eager to embrace technology's conveniences.

Organizing Your Inbox

Organizing your inbox effectively can transform the way you interact with your email, making it a tool of efficiency rather than a source of stress. The key to mastering your inbox lies in understanding the various features and functions that Windows 11 offers for email organization. **Folders** and **categories** are your first line of defense in keeping your emails sorted. By creating folders for different projects, contacts, or types of communication, you can file away emails in a manner that makes them easy to retrieve when needed. Similarly, assigning categories or tags to emails allows for quick filtering, so you can view all emails related to a specific topic or project at once.

The **search function** in your email application is a powerful tool for finding specific emails when you remember details such as the sender's name, a keyword from the subject line, or a phrase from the email body. Learning to use advanced search queries can significantly reduce the time spent hunting for old emails. For instance, searching for from:john@example.com will show all emails sent from John's email address, while subject:"meeting agenda" will bring up emails with that exact phrase in the subject line.

Rules are another feature that can automate the organization of your inbox. By setting up rules, you can have emails from certain senders, with specific subjects, or containing particular keywords automatically moved to a designated folder, marked as important, or even deleted. This automation can help in managing the influx of emails, ensuring that important messages stand out and less critical ones do not clutter your main inbox view.

Archiving emails rather than deleting them is a practice that can help keep your inbox clean while still retaining access to old communications. Archived emails are moved out of your main inbox but remain searchable, providing a compromise between decluttering and data retention.

Finally, regular **maintenance** of your inbox is crucial. Dedicate time each week to review your folders and categories, update your rules based on new email patterns, and archive or delete old emails that are no longer needed. This ongoing process will help keep your inbox manageable and make email communication more effective.

By leveraging folders, categories, the search function, rules, and archiving, along with a commitment to regular inbox maintenance, you can achieve an organized and efficient email experience on Windows 11. These strategies not only reduce the time spent managing emails but also enhance your overall productivity and ease of communication.

Staying Safe Online

In the digital age, **staying safe online** is paramount, especially for seniors who may be more vulnerable to cyber threats. One of the first steps in safeguarding your online experience is to **create strong passwords**. A strong password should be a mix of letters, numbers, and special characters, making it difficult for hackers to guess. Consider using a **password manager** to keep track of your passwords securely. These tools not only store your passwords in an encrypted format but also generate strong passwords for you.

Another critical aspect of online safety is being aware of **phishing scams**. Phishing is a technique used by cybercriminals to trick you into revealing personal information, such as bank account numbers or passwords. Be cautious of emails or messages that urge immediate action, request sensitive information, or contain suspicious links. Always verify the authenticity of the request by contacting the company directly through official channels.

Updating your software and operating system regularly is crucial in protecting your computer from new vulnerabilities. Windows 11 provides automatic updates, but you should periodically check to ensure these updates are being applied successfully. These updates often include patches for security flaws that could be exploited by malware or hackers.

Using antivirus software is another essential layer of protection. Windows 11 comes with built-in antivirus protection through Windows Security. However, you may consider additional antivirus software for more comprehensive coverage. Ensure that your antivirus is always up to date and perform regular scans to detect and remove any malicious software.

Be mindful of the **privacy settings** on websites and social media platforms. Adjust these settings to limit what information is public and who can see your posts. This can help protect your personal information from being accessed by strangers.

Lastly, **backing up your data** regularly can save you from potential cyber threats like ransomware. Use an external hard drive or cloud storage services to create copies of your important files. This way, if your computer is ever compromised, you won't lose everything.

By following these guidelines, you can significantly reduce your risk of falling victim to online threats. Remember, staying informed and cautious is your best defense against the evolving landscape of cyber security threats.

Recognizing and Avoiding Scams

In the realm of cyber security, understanding the nuances of scam recognition is crucial. Scammers have become increasingly sophisticated, employing tactics that can sometimes bypass even the most vigilant of users. The cornerstone of avoiding scams lies in recognizing the signs of a fraudulent communication or offer. Often, scams will present themselves through unsolicited emails, messages, or pop-up ads, purporting to be from reputable entities with offers that seem too good to be true or urgent requests for personal information. It's essential to scrutinize any communication that asks for sensitive information like social security numbers, bank account details, or login credentials. A legitimate company will never ask for this information via email or text message.

Another prevalent scamming technique is the use of fear or urgency to provoke immediate action. This could manifest as a message claiming your account has been compromised and urging you to click a link to secure it. Instead of clicking through, directly contact the institution through official channels to verify the claim. Additionally, be wary of any requests for payment through untraceable methods like gift cards or wire transfers, as these are red flags for fraudulent activity.

To further safeguard against scams, consider implementing technical measures such as spam filters on your email accounts and ad blockers on your web browsers. These tools can significantly reduce the volume of potentially harmful content reaching you. Moreover, regularly updating your software and operating system ensures that security patches are applied, closing vulnerabilities that could be exploited by scammers.

Educating oneself on the latest scamming techniques is also invaluable. Scammers continually evolve their methods, so staying informed through reputable sources can provide you with the knowledge to spot and avoid new types of scams. Websites like the Federal Trade Commission (FTC) offer resources and alerts on current scams affecting consumers.

For those instances where you suspect you've encountered a scam, it's important to know how to respond. First, do not engage with the scammer. If you've received an email, do not reply, click on any links, or download attachments. Report the scam to the appropriate authorities, such as the FTC, and inform your contacts if your email account was compromised. Taking these steps helps not only in protecting yourself but also in preventing the spread of scams to others.

Incorporating these practices into your daily online activities can significantly enhance your ability to recognize and avoid scams. By exercising caution and staying informed, you can navigate the internet more securely, keeping your personal information and finances safe from fraudulent entities.

Creating Strong Passwords

Creating strong passwords is an essential skill in maintaining online security, especially for seniors who are increasingly embracing digital technologies for various needs, from banking to social interactions. The complexity and uniqueness of a password can significantly deter unauthorized access to personal accounts, making it a first line of defense against cyber threats. A robust password combines letters (both uppercase and lowercase), numbers, and special characters in a sequence that is not easily guessed by humans or decipherable by computer algorithms. The length of the password also plays a critical role, with a minimum of 12 characters recommended for enhanced security.

One effective strategy for generating and remembering complex passwords is the use of mnemonic devices or phrases. For instance, the sentence "My dog Baxter eats 2 bananas on Fridays!" can be transformed into a password by taking the first letter of each word and including the numbers and punctuation, resulting in MdB e2b oF!. This method creates a password that is both complex and memorable. However, even with mnemonic techniques, remembering multiple strong passwords for different accounts can be challenging.

This is where password managers become invaluable tools. A password manager securely stores all your passwords in an encrypted database, requiring you to remember only one master password to access the rest. Many password managers also offer the functionality to generate strong, random passwords for each of your accounts, ensuring that each password is unique and meets security requirements. This eliminates the need for you to come up with and remember multiple complex passwords, simplifying your online security without compromising it.

For additional security, enable two-factor authentication (2FA) wherever possible. This adds another layer of protection by requiring a second form of verification beyond your password, such as a code sent to your mobile device. Even if a hacker manages to decipher your password, without the second factor, they cannot gain access to your account.

Regularly updating your passwords is another key practice. Change your passwords periodically, and especially after a service has experienced a security breach. This helps to ensure that even if your data was compromised, the information cannot be used for future unauthorized access.

In the context of Windows 11, leveraging the built-in security features such as Windows Hello can offer a more personal and secure way to log in to your device without the need for a traditional password. Windows Hello uses facial recognition, fingerprint, or a PIN as alternatives to passwords, providing both convenience and enhanced security.

By adopting these practices, seniors can significantly bolster their online security, protecting their personal information from unauthorized access. With the increasing prevalence of cyber threats, taking proactive steps to secure online accounts through strong, unique passwords, and utilizing additional security measures like password managers and two-factor authentication, is more important than ever.

Using Antivirus Software

Antivirus software serves as a critical defense mechanism against various forms of malware, including viruses, spyware, ransomware, and phishing attacks. For seniors navigating the complexities of Windows 11, understanding how to effectively use antivirus software is paramount to maintaining a secure computing environment. Windows 11 is equipped with Windows Security, a built-in antivirus feature that provides comprehensive protection against threats. However, the landscape of cyber threats is ever-evolving, necessitating additional layers of security to safeguard sensitive information and ensure a safe online experience.

To enhance your protection, consider installing reputable third-party antivirus software. These programs offer advanced features such as real-time scanning, automatic updates, and heuristic analysis to detect and neutralize threats based on behavior. When selecting antivirus software, prioritize solutions that are known for their efficacy, minimal impact on system performance, and compatibility with Windows 11. Installation is typically straightforward, involving downloading the software from the provider's website and following the on-screen instructions. Once installed, configure the software to perform automatic scans and updates, ensuring your system is protected against the latest threats.

Regularly scanning your computer for malware is a critical practice. Schedule full system scans at least once a week and perform manual scans if you suspect your computer has been compromised. If malware is detected, the antivirus software will attempt to quarantine or delete the infected files, mitigating the risk of data loss or further infection. Be vigilant about monitoring the antivirus software's notifications and take immediate action if a threat is detected.

In addition to using antivirus software, adopt safe browsing habits to further reduce your risk of infection. Avoid clicking on suspicious links, downloading attachments from unknown sources, and visiting unsecured websites. These behaviors are common vectors for malware and can compromise your computer's security even with antivirus protection in place.

Updating your antivirus software is as crucial as updating Windows 11 itself. Cybercriminals continually develop new methods to exploit vulnerabilities, and antivirus providers regularly release updates to counter these threats. Ensure that your antivirus software is set to update automatically, providing you with the most current protection available.

For seniors seeking to maximize their security on Windows 11, integrating the use of antivirus software with other security practices offers a robust defense against cyber threats. By understanding the importance of antivirus protection, regularly updating software, and practicing safe browsing habits, seniors can confidently navigate the digital world with a significantly reduced risk of encountering malicious software.

Chapter 3: Apps and the Microsoft Store

Discovering and installing new apps on Windows 11 can significantly enhance your computing experience, allowing you to tailor the system to your personal needs and interests. The Microsoft Store is the central hub for finding, purchasing, and downloading a wide variety of applications ranging from productivity tools to games and entertainment apps. To begin, click on the Microsoft Store icon on the taskbar or search for it using the search box on the taskbar. Once the Store app is open, you'll be greeted with a user-friendly interface showcasing featured apps, deals, and collections. Navigating the Microsoft Store is straightforward. The homepage provides quick access to various categories such as **Gaming**, **Entertainment**, **Productivity**, and **Education**. You can click on any category to explore its offerings or use the search bar at the top of the window to find specific apps by name.

When you find an app that interests you, click on its listing to view more details, including descriptions, screenshots, and user reviews. This information can be invaluable in helping you decide whether an app meets your needs and expectations. Pay particular attention to the **System Requirements** section to ensure the app is compatible with your device. To download an app, simply click the **Get** or **Buy** button, depending on whether the app is free or paid. If it's your first time making a purchase, you may be prompted to enter payment information or redeem a gift card.

The Microsoft Store also offers a selection of apps specifically designed to enhance accessibility, such as screen readers, magnification software, and apps that simplify navigation for users with mobility challenges. Exploring these options can make your Windows 11 experience more comfortable and personalized.

After installing an app, you'll find it listed in the Start menu, where you can pin it to the Start menu or taskbar for easy access. Managing your apps is also a breeze. The Microsoft Store keeps track of all your app downloads, making it easy to update them when new versions are released. To check for updates, click on the **Library** icon at the bottom left corner of the Store app and then select **Get updates**. Keeping your apps up to date ensures that you have the latest features and security improvements.

For those interested in productivity, the Microsoft Store offers a wide array of apps designed to help you stay organized, manage your time, and work more efficiently. From note-taking apps like Microsoft OneNote to project management tools and office suites, there's something for everyone. Social and communication apps are also plentiful, allowing you to stay connected with friends, family, and colleagues through video calls, messaging, and social networking.

For those with a creative flair, the Microsoft Store is a treasure trove of apps that cater to various artistic pursuits. Whether you're interested in digital painting, photo editing, or music production, there's a wide selection of apps available to unleash your creativity. Adobe Photoshop Elements, for example, offers powerful image editing capabilities, while FL Studio Mobile lets you produce music directly on your Windows 11 device. Exploring these apps can open up new hobbies or even enhance your professional skills in graphic design, photography, or music.

Gamers will find the Microsoft Store to be a gateway to countless hours of entertainment, with a vast library of games spanning all genres. From casual games that are perfect for quick sessions to immersive AAA titles that offer deep, engaging experiences, the Microsoft Store has something for every type of gamer. Additionally, with Xbox integration, some games support cross-play and achievements, enriching the gaming experience on Windows 11.

Reading enthusiasts aren't left out either. The Microsoft Store provides access to a variety of apps for reading eBooks, magazines, and comics. Apps like Kindle and Audible bring vast libraries of books and audiobooks to your fingertips, making it easy to enjoy your favorite reads or discover new ones. For those interested in staying updated with the latest news, apps like Microsoft News deliver personalized news feeds, ensuring you're always informed about the topics that matter most to you.

The Microsoft Store isn't just about individual apps; it's also a platform for enhancing the functionality of your device through various utilities and tools. From antivirus software to system optimization tools, you can find apps to keep your Windows 11 running smoothly and securely. Utilities like Norton Antivirus and CCleaner are available to protect your device from malware and keep it performing at its best.

In addition to the wealth of apps available, the Microsoft Store offers a level of security and peace of mind that comes from knowing that all apps have been vetted by Microsoft. This means you can download and use apps with confidence, knowing they meet a standard of quality and security. This is particularly reassuring for those who may be apprehensive about downloading software from the internet.

Finally, the Microsoft Store is continuously evolving, with new apps and features being added regularly. This dynamic nature ensures that the platform remains relevant and valuable to users, providing a consistent stream of new content and functionality to explore. Whether you're looking to increase productivity, explore new hobbies, or simply enhance your Windows 11 experience, the Microsoft Store is an essential resource that offers something for everyone.

Discovering Useful Apps

In the realm of Windows 11, the Microsoft Store serves as a treasure trove of applications designed to enhance productivity, foster communication, and entertain. For seniors embarking on the digital adventure, identifying apps that resonate with their lifestyle, interests, and needs is crucial. Among the plethora of options, productivity apps like Microsoft Office, which includes Word, Excel, and PowerPoint, stand out for their utility in document creation, data management, and presentation design. These apps are indispensable for managing personal projects, organizing family events, or even exploring new hobbies such as writing or genealogy.

Social and communication apps also play a pivotal role in staying connected with loved ones and the world. Skype and Microsoft Teams, for instance, offer video calling and messaging services that bridge the gap between friends and family members, irrespective of the distance. These platforms are user-friendly and allow for real-time interaction, making them ideal for seniors keen on maintaining social ties.

For those with a penchant for creativity, the Microsoft Store presents apps like Paint 3D and Adobe Photoshop Elements. Paint 3D, with its intuitive interface, enables users to delve into the world of 3D modeling without the need for complex training. Adobe Photoshop Elements, on the other hand, caters to photo editing enthusiasts looking to enhance their digital photographs with professional-grade tools.

Entertainment is another domain where the Microsoft Store excels. Apps like Netflix, Spotify, and Audible offer access to a vast array of movies, music, and audiobooks, catering to diverse tastes and preferences. These services require subscriptions, but they often provide free trials for new users, allowing seniors to explore their offerings before committing financially.

Navigating the Microsoft Store might seem daunting at first, but it's designed with ease of use in mind. To find an app, simply use the search bar at the top of the Store window and type in the name or category of the app you're looking for. Once you've found an app that interests you, click on it to view more details, including user reviews, which can provide valuable insights into the app's functionality and user experience.

Installing an app is straightforward: click the Get button, and Windows 11 will handle the rest, downloading and installing the app on your computer. It's advisable to regularly check for updates to your apps, ensuring you have the latest features and security enhancements. This can be done by clicking on the Library button in the Microsoft Store and selecting Get updates.

In summary, the Microsoft Store is a gateway to enriching your digital life with useful and entertaining apps. Whether you're looking to streamline your day-to-day tasks, stay in touch with family and friends, unleash your creativity, or simply enjoy your leisure time, there's an app for almost every need and interest.

Productivity Apps

Beyond the basic utilities, the Microsoft Store offers a suite of productivity apps tailored to enhance efficiency and streamline the workflow for seniors. One such indispensable tool is **OneNote**, a digital notebook that allows for the organization of thoughts, ideas, and schedules in one easily accessible place. Its user-friendly interface encourages the jotting down of notes, compiling of research, and even the storing of web articles for later review. With features like handwriting recognition and audio note capabilities, OneNote caters to various input preferences, making it a versatile app for personal and professional use.

Outlook, another critical app, goes beyond mere email management. It integrates calendar, task lists, and contact information, creating a comprehensive system for managing day-to-day activities. Its filtering and sorting functions help in prioritizing emails and events, ensuring that important dates and communications do not get overlooked. For seniors managing a busy schedule or keeping track of family events, Outlook's intuitive design and synchronization across devices make it a central hub for personal organization.

In the realm of financial management, **Excel** stands out as a powerful tool for budgeting and tracking expenses. With a range of templates designed for users at any expertise level, seniors can easily begin organizing their financial life, from simple expense tracking to more complex retirement planning. Excel's functions and formulas process data efficiently, offering insights and summaries through charts and tables, thus demystifying financial planning for those who may not have a background in finance.

For creative writing and document preparation, **Word** offers a robust platform with features that cater to both novice and experienced writers. Its spell check and grammar suggestions aid in producing polished texts, while advanced layout options allow for the creation of professional documents. Whether drafting a family newsletter, compiling a recipe book, or writing memoirs, Word provides the flexibility and tools necessary to bring creative projects to life.

Lastly, **PowerPoint** emerges as a key app for those looking to share stories, present ideas, or teach skills. With its user-friendly interface, seniors can design compelling presentations using templates, animations, and multimedia integration. This app not only facilitates the sharing of knowledge and experiences but also encourages the development of new digital skills in a supportive, creative environment.

Each of these productivity apps, available through the Microsoft Store, is designed with the user in mind, offering tutorials and support to guide seniors through the learning process. The integration of these apps into daily routines can significantly enhance productivity, organization, and creative expression, empowering seniors to harness the full potential of Windows 11 for their personal and professional growth.

Social and Communication Apps

In the digital age, the ability to stay connected with family, friends, and the community is invaluable, especially for seniors who may find themselves more isolated than they once were. The Microsoft Store, accessible through Windows 11, offers a variety of social and communication apps designed to bridge these gaps, fostering connections and facilitating conversations across the globe. Among these, WhatsApp and Facebook Messenger stand out for their widespread use and intuitive interfaces, making them excellent choices for seniors eager to maintain active social lives.

WhatsApp offers end-to-end encrypted messaging, voice, and video calls, ensuring that conversations remain private and secure. Its group chat feature is particularly useful for organizing family gatherings or staying in touch with groups of friends, allowing for the sharing of photos, videos, and documents with ease. The app's simplicity does not require extensive technical knowledge, making it accessible for users who may not be as familiar with digital communication tools.

Facebook Messenger, another powerful tool in the arsenal of social apps, integrates seamlessly with Facebook's social network, providing a convenient way to chat with friends, join interest groups, or follow news and events. Its video call feature supports real-time face-to-face communication, bringing loved ones closer despite physical distance. Messenger also offers a variety of interactive elements such as stickers, GIFs, and reaction emojis, adding a playful dimension to conversations and making digital communication more engaging.

For seniors looking to expand their social circles or explore new interests, Meetup is an app that connects individuals with groups and events in their local area based on shared interests. Whether it's hiking, painting, technology, or books, Meetup provides a platform to meet like-minded people and engage in activities together. This app not only encourages social interaction but also promotes physical activity and mental engagement, contributing to a healthier, more fulfilling lifestyle.

In addition to these, the Microsoft Store also features apps like Zoom and Google Meet, which have become indispensable for video conferencing. These apps have transcended their original business-oriented purposes, becoming lifelines for families to celebrate birthdays, holidays, and other milestones virtually. Their user-friendly interfaces allow seniors to participate in these gatherings without the need for complex setups, ensuring they're never out of reach for those important moments.

Each of these apps, while serving the primary purpose of communication, also offers unique features that cater to the diverse needs and preferences of seniors. From ensuring security and privacy with encrypted messages to enabling participation in community events and family gatherings, these tools play a crucial role in enhancing the quality of life for seniors by keeping them connected and engaged.

To get started with any of these apps, simply navigate to the Microsoft Store on your Windows 11 device, use the search function to find the app you're interested in, and click Get to download and install it. Once installed, you'll typically be prompted to create an account or log in, a process that's usually straightforward and guided step-by-step within the app itself. Remember, staying connected in the digital age is not just about technology; it's about enriching lives with meaningful interactions and experiences, all of which are made possible through these social and communication apps available at your fingertips.

Installing and Managing Apps

Once you've navigated the Microsoft Store and found an app that piques your interest, the next step is to install it. Clicking on the `Get` button will initiate the download and installation process. However, managing these apps post-installation is equally important to ensure your system remains organized and up-to-date. Here are some key points to consider:

- **Updating Apps**: Keeping your apps updated is crucial for security and functionality. Windows 11 simplifies this process through the Microsoft Store. Navigate to the `Library` section within the Store, where you'll find an `Get updates` button. Clicking this will check for updates across all your installed apps, downloading and installing any available updates automatically. This feature ensures that you're always using the latest versions, which include the newest features and security patches.

- **Uninstalling Apps**: Over time, you may find certain apps no longer serve your needs or you simply wish to declutter your digital space. Uninstalling apps in Windows 11 is straightforward. Press the `Windows` key to bring up the Start menu, find the app you wish to remove, right-click on it, and select `Uninstall`. Confirm your decision if prompted, and Windows will remove the app from your system. This process helps in managing storage space and ensuring your system remains optimized.

- **App Settings and Permissions**: After installing an app, you might need to adjust its settings or permissions to suit your preferences or enhance security. Most apps will prompt you to grant certain permissions upon first launch, such as access to your microphone, camera, or location. It's important to review these requests carefully and only grant permissions that are necessary for the app's functionality. You can always adjust these settings later by going to `Settings` > `Privacy & Security` > `App Permissions` on your Windows 11 device.

- **Troubleshooting Apps**: Occasionally, you may encounter issues with an app not functioning as expected. Before reaching out for technical support, there are a few troubleshooting steps you can take. First, check if there are any updates available for the app, as mentioned earlier. If the issue persists, try uninstalling and then reinstalling the app. This can often resolve minor glitches or errors. Additionally, consult the app's help section or online forums for specific troubleshooting tips related to the app.

- **Organizing Apps**: As you install more apps, organizing them can help maintain an efficient workflow. You can group related apps together on the Start menu by dragging one app over another to create a folder. Naming these folders according to categories, such as `Productivity`, `Social`, or `Entertainment`, can make it easier to find what you're looking for at a glance.

By following these guidelines, you can effectively manage your apps on Windows 11, ensuring a smooth and productive experience. Regularly updating and auditing your app collection not only enhances security but also optimizes your device's performance, allowing you to focus on enjoying the benefits of your digital life.

Navigating the Microsoft Store

The Microsoft Store, integral to enhancing the Windows 11 experience, offers a myriad of apps designed to cater to diverse needs and interests. For seniors looking to enrich their digital journey, understanding how to effectively manage these applications is key. The process of updating apps is streamlined within the Microsoft Store, ensuring that users have access to the latest features and security improvements. By navigating to the `Library` section and selecting the `Get updates` button, Windows 11 diligently checks for and installs any available updates across all installed apps. This proactive approach not only secures the digital environment but also enhances app functionality, providing a seamless user experience.

In the digital landscape, the relevance of apps can evolve, leading to the occasional need to uninstall applications that are no longer useful or to declutter the digital workspace. Windows 11 simplifies this process, allowing users to easily remove unwanted apps. By pressing the `Windows` key, accessing the Start menu, right-clicking on the undesired app, and selecting `Uninstall`, users can efficiently manage their app inventory, freeing up space and resources on their device.

Adjusting app settings and permissions post-installation is crucial for optimizing app performance and safeguarding personal privacy. Upon initial launch, most apps request permissions to access certain device functionalities, such as the microphone, camera, or location services. It is imperative for users to scrutinize these requests, granting permissions only when necessary for the app's operation. Adjustments to these permissions can be made at any time within the `Settings` > `Privacy & Security` > `App Permissions` section of Windows 11, ensuring users maintain control over their digital footprint.

Encountering issues with apps is not uncommon, and Windows 11 provides users with tools to troubleshoot and resolve such problems independently. Should an app not perform as expected, checking for updates or reinstalling the app can often rectify the issue. Additionally, the app's help section or online forums may offer solutions tailored to specific concerns, empowering users to address challenges without external assistance.

Organizing apps effectively can significantly enhance the user experience, making navigation and access more intuitive. Windows 11 facilitates this by allowing users to group related apps into folders directly from the Start menu, enabling a more organized and streamlined interface. Labeling these folders according to categories such as `Productivity`, `Social`, or `Entertainment` can further simplify app management, allowing for quick and easy access to desired applications.

By embracing these strategies for installing, updating, and managing apps through the Microsoft Store, seniors can confidently navigate Windows 11, making the most of their devices. Regularly updating apps, judiciously managing installations, adjusting settings for optimal performance and privacy, troubleshooting as needed, and organizing apps for ease of use are all practices that contribute to a more enjoyable and productive digital experience. With these tools and techniques, the Microsoft Store becomes not just a marketplace for applications but a gateway to enhancing the functionality and enjoyment of Windows 11, tailored to the unique needs and preferences of each user

Updating and Uninstalling Apps

Managing the lifecycle of apps on your Windows 11 device is a critical aspect of maintaining both system performance and security. Regular updates not only introduce new features but also patch vulnerabilities that could compromise your digital safety. Conversely, uninstalling apps that are no longer needed can free up valuable disk space and resources, contributing to a smoother computing experience.

When it comes to **updating apps**, the Microsoft Store automates much of the process, yet a proactive approach ensures that no update slips through the cracks. Periodically, it's advisable to manually check for updates by navigating to the `Library` section of the Microsoft Store and selecting the `Get updates` button. This action prompts Windows 11 to scan for and apply any available updates across your installed apps. It's a straightforward process that plays a pivotal role in optimizing app functionality and fortifying security.

For apps installed outside of the Microsoft Store, it's important to enable any built-in update mechanisms these apps may offer. Many applications will automatically check for updates upon launch, but others might require a visit to the app's settings or help menu to initiate an update check. For example, to update a third-party app manually, you might navigate to its `Help` menu and select `Check for Updates`. If an update is available, follow the on-screen instructions to download and install it. This method ensures that even non-Store apps benefit from the latest improvements and security patches.

Uninstalling apps that are no longer in use is equally important. For apps downloaded from the Microsoft Store, the process is as simple as pressing the `Windows` key, searching for the app by name, right-clicking on the app's icon, and selecting `Uninstall`. A confirmation dialog will appear, and once confirmed, Windows will proceed to remove the app from your system. This method is effective for decluttering your Start menu and freeing up system resources.

For applications installed from sources other than the Microsoft Store, the uninstallation process might differ slightly. Accessing the `Settings` app, then navigating to `Apps` > `Apps & features`, presents a list of all installed applications. Locating the app in question and selecting `Uninstall` will initiate the removal process. Some applications may provide a custom uninstallation utility, which can be accessed from the same location or through the app's installation folder.

Adjusting **app settings and permissions** is a critical step following installation. Windows 11 offers comprehensive control over what resources an app can access, such as your camera, microphone, or location data. To adjust these permissions, open `Settings`, go to `Privacy & Security`, and select `App Permissions`. Here, you can review and modify the permissions for each app, ensuring they only have access to what's necessary for their operation. Being judicious with app permissions not only enhances privacy but also minimizes potential security risks.

Troubleshooting app performance issues occasionally requires more than just updating or reinstalling. If an app is not performing as expected, consulting the `Event Viewer` in Windows 11 can offer insights into application errors or system warnings related to the app. Accessing `Event Viewer` is done by right-clicking the Start button, selecting `Run`, typing `eventvwr.msc`, and pressing Enter. Navigating to `Windows Logs` > `Application` reveals a log of application events, where errors associated with the problematic app can be investigated further.

Organizing apps effectively can enhance your productivity and overall user experience. Grouping apps by function or frequency of use on the Start menu or Taskbar allows for quick access. For instance, you might group all productivity apps like Word, Excel, and Outlook together, creating a cohesive workspace that facilitates focus and efficiency. Customizing these groups according to personal workflow preferences or projects at hand can streamline your computing experience, making it more intuitive and aligned with your daily tasks.

By embracing these practices for updating, uninstalling, and managing apps, you can ensure that your Windows 11 system remains secure, efficient, and tailored to your specific needs. Regular maintenance, combined with a strategic approach to app management, empowers you to leverage the full potential of your device, enhancing both productivity and enjoyment.

Entertainment on Windows 11

For those eager to dive into the world of **entertainment on Windows 11**, the platform offers a rich tapestry of applications and features designed to cater to a wide range of interests. From **streaming music and videos** to **reading eBooks and news**, Windows 11 stands as a central hub for digital leisure.

Streaming Music and Videos: Windows 11 integrates seamlessly with popular services like **Spotify** and **Netflix**, allowing users to access a vast library of songs, albums, movies, and TV shows. To enhance your experience, consider exploring the Microsoft Store for apps like **VLC Media Player** for playing various media formats or **Kodi** for a more customizable media center experience. Remember, downloading these apps is straightforward: simply search for the app in the Microsoft Store and click Install.

Reading eBooks and News: For those who enjoy reading, the **Microsoft News** app provides a curated selection of the latest news stories from around the world. Additionally, the **Kindle** app can be downloaded from the Microsoft Store, offering access to Amazon's extensive collection of eBooks. The app's interface is designed to be senior-friendly, with options to adjust font size and background color for a more comfortable reading experience.

To access these entertainment options, navigate to the **Microsoft Store** by clicking on its icon in the taskbar or searching for it in the Start menu. Once there, use the search bar at the top of the window to find the desired app. After installation, you can find your new apps listed in the Start menu, ready to launch.

For those interested in staying current with the latest news or diving into a good book, setting up **live tiles** for news apps or the Kindle app on the Start menu can provide quick access to new content right from your desktop. To do this, right-click on the app in the Start menu and select Pin to Start.

In conclusion, Windows 11 offers a plethora of entertainment options that cater to diverse interests. Whether you're looking to unwind with your favorite music, catch up on the latest movies and TV shows, or lose yourself in a good book, Windows 11 provides the tools and apps to enrich your leisure time. Remember, exploring the Microsoft Store can unveil even more apps to enhance your entertainment experience, making your time on Windows 11 both enjoyable and fulfilling.

Streaming Music and Videos

For seniors eager to immerse themselves in the world of digital entertainment, **Windows 11** provides an intuitive platform for streaming music and videos, offering access to a plethora of content that caters to every taste and interest. With services like **Spotify** for music and **Netflix** for movies and TV shows already highlighted, it's essential to delve deeper into the functionalities that make these services user-friendly and accessible. For instance, Spotify allows users to create personalized playlists and discover new music through its "Discover Weekly" feature, a testament to the platform's commitment to tailoring user experience. Similarly, Netflix's recommendation system learns from your viewing habits, suggesting new titles based on your preferences.

Beyond these well-known giants, Windows 11 also supports a variety of other streaming services through applications available in the **Microsoft Store**. **Hulu**, **Amazon Prime Video**, and **Disney+** are just a few examples of apps that offer unique libraries of content, including original series, classic films, and new releases. Installing these apps follows the same simple process: search, select, and click Install. Once installed, these services integrate smoothly with Windows 11, allowing for easy access directly from the Start menu or taskbar, depending on your personal setup preferences.

For music enthusiasts interested in exploring beyond Spotify, **Pandora** and **Tidal** offer compelling alternatives. Pandora shines with its personalized internet radio service, creating stations based on artists or songs you love. Tidal, on the other hand, appeals to audiophiles with its high-fidelity sound quality and exclusive content. Both services have apps available in the Microsoft Store, ensuring a straightforward setup process.

Exploring these streaming services on Windows 11, seniors can take advantage of features designed to enhance their listening and viewing experiences. For example, many apps support offline playback, allowing you to download your favorite tracks, albums, or episodes to enjoy without an internet connection. This feature is particularly useful for those with limited data plans or when traveling to areas with poor internet connectivity.

Moreover, the integration of **Cortana**, Windows 11's built-in digital assistant, offers an additional layer of convenience. By setting up Cortana, you can use voice commands to play music, pause videos, or search for new content, all without needing to navigate through apps manually. This hands-free control is not only practical but also aligns with the needs of seniors looking for simpler, more accessible ways to enjoy technology.

Accessibility features within Windows 11 further enhance the entertainment experience for seniors. High contrast themes, screen magnifiers, and closed captions are available across the operating system, ensuring that everyone, regardless of visual or hearing impairments, can enjoy streaming content comfortably. These settings are easily adjustable from the Ease of Access Center, demonstrating Windows 11's commitment to inclusivity.

In embracing the entertainment possibilities offered by Windows 11, seniors can discover a world of music, movies, and TV shows at their fingertips. Whether it's revisiting classic hits, catching up on missed episodes of a favorite series, or exploring new genres, the combination of user-friendly streaming services and Windows 11's accessible design ensures a fulfilling and enjoyable digital entertainment experience.

Reading eBooks and News

The digital age has transformed the way we consume literature and stay informed, with eBooks and online news becoming increasingly popular. For seniors looking to delve into the vast world of digital reading, Windows 11 provides an accessible gateway. The Kindle app, available through the Microsoft Store, is an exemplary tool for accessing a wide range of eBooks. With its user-friendly interface, the app allows users to easily search for titles, purchase books, or borrow from a vast library if they are Amazon Prime members. The customization options available within the Kindle app are particularly beneficial for seniors, allowing for adjustments in font size and background color to ensure a comfortable reading experience without straining the eyes.

Furthermore, the Microsoft News app stands as a reliable source for staying updated with the latest global events. This app aggregates news from reputable sources, offering a diverse range of viewpoints and topics. Users can personalize their news feed by selecting areas of interest, ensuring that they receive news that is most relevant to them. The app also allows for the adjustment of text size, making it easier for those with vision impairments to stay informed.

For seniors interested in a broader range of reading materials, the Microsoft Store offers various other apps designed for reading eBooks and news. Apps like Audible are perfect for those who prefer audiobooks, providing access to a vast collection of titles that can be listened to anytime, anywhere. This is particularly advantageous for individuals who may have difficulty reading small text or those who simply enjoy the convenience of listening to books while engaging in other activities.

RSS feed readers are another valuable tool for seniors wanting to consolidate news and articles from multiple sources into one easy-to-navigate location. Apps like Feedly allow users to subscribe to their favorite news outlets, blogs, and online magazines, keeping all their reading material in one place. This eliminates the need to visit multiple websites to stay informed, simplifying the process of consuming online content.

Incorporating these digital tools into daily routines can significantly enhance the reading and news consumption experience for seniors. By leveraging the capabilities of Windows 11 and the apps available through the Microsoft Store, seniors can easily access a wealth of information and literature tailored to their preferences and needs. This not only keeps them connected with the world but also supports lifelong learning and entertainment. With these resources at their fingertips, seniors are empowered to explore new topics, indulge in their favorite hobbies, and stay engaged with current events, all from the comfort of their home.

Chapter 4: Files and Folders

Managing files and folders in Windows 11 is a fundamental skill that enhances your computing experience, ensuring that you can organize, access, and protect your digital documents with ease. The operating system introduces several tools and features designed to streamline file management, making it more intuitive for users, especially seniors who might be managing a vast array of documents, photos, and other files. **File Explorer** is at the heart of Windows 11's file management system, acting as the gateway to all your stored data. It allows you to view, open, move, copy, rename, and delete files and folders across different locations, including your hard drive, connected external devices, and cloud storage services like **OneDrive**.

Creating and Organizing Folders: To begin organizing your files, it's essential to understand how to create new folders. Right-click on an empty space within File Explorer, select `New`, then `Folder`, and give it a descriptive name that reflects its contents. This simple act of categorization can significantly aid in locating specific documents or media in the future. For more advanced organization, consider nesting folders within each other to create a hierarchy of categories and subcategories, mirroring the way you might organize physical documents in a filing cabinet.

Copying and Moving Files: When you need to rearrange your digital documents, Windows 11 makes it straightforward with its drag-and-drop functionality. To move a file, simply click and hold the file, then drag it to the desired folder and release. If you wish to copy the file instead, hold down the `Ctrl` key while you drag and drop. This method is particularly useful for organizing files without creating unnecessary duplicates. For operations involving multiple files, select them by holding the `Ctrl` key and clicking on each file, then use the right-click menu to choose `Copy` or `Move to` options.

Deleting Files: Managing your digital clutter is just as important as organizing. To delete a file or folder, right-click it and select `Delete`, or press the `Delete` key on your keyboard. Deleted items are moved to the **Recycle Bin**, where they are stored temporarily, allowing you to recover them if needed. It's a good practice to periodically review the contents of your Recycle Bin and permanently delete items to free up storage space.

Searching for Files: Windows 11's search functionality within File Explorer has been enhanced to make finding files an effortless task. Simply type the name of the document or a keyword in the search box at the top-right corner of the File Explorer window. The system will quickly filter through your files, presenting you with a list of matches. This feature is invaluable for locating specific files among a large collection, saving time and frustration.

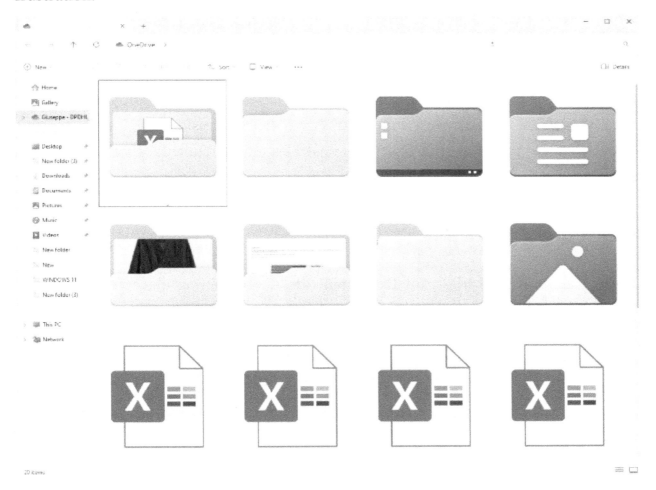

OneDrive Integration: For seniors looking to safeguard their data against hardware failures or to access files across multiple devices, OneDrive offers a seamless cloud storage solution. By saving files to OneDrive, you not only back them up online but also make them accessible from any device with an internet connection. Windows 11 integrates OneDrive directly into File Explorer, making it easy to manage your cloud-stored files alongside those on your local drive. To set up OneDrive, look for its icon in the taskbar's notification area or within File Explorer, and follow the prompts to sign in with your Microsoft account.

In the next section, we will delve deeper into the advanced features of file management, including shortcuts for efficiency, using tags and metadata for organization, and setting up file sharing for collaboration. These tools and techniques will further empower you to take control of your digital environment, ensuring that your files are not only well-organized but also easily accessible and secure.

Shortcuts for Efficiency: Mastering keyboard shortcuts can significantly enhance your file management efficiency in Windows 11. For instance, pressing `Ctrl` + `C` to copy, `Ctrl` + `V` to paste, and `Ctrl` + `X` to cut files are fundamental shortcuts that can save time during file organization. Additionally, using `Ctrl` + `Z` to undo the last action offers a quick way to correct mistakes. For those who manage large volumes of files, learning these shortcuts can be a game-changer in streamlining your workflow.

Using Tags and Metadata for Organization: Another powerful feature of Windows 11 is the ability to add tags and metadata to files. This is particularly useful for photos and documents, as it allows you to categorize files in ways that are meaningful to you. For example, you can tag photos with the names of people or places, making them easier to find later. To add tags to a file, right-click it, select `Properties`, go to the `Details` tab, and enter your tags in the `Tags` field. Utilizing tags and metadata can transform your file searching capabilities, enabling you to locate files based on content characteristics rather than just file names.

Setting Up File Sharing for Collaboration: Windows 11 simplifies the process of sharing files with others, making it an ideal platform for collaboration. Whether you're sharing photos with family or documents with a study group, you can use File Explorer to share files via OneDrive or a local network. To share a file, right-click it, select `Share`, and choose an app to share through or select `Specific people` if you're sharing over a network. This feature ensures that you can easily collaborate on projects or share memories with loved ones, all within a secure environment.

File Backup and Recovery Options: Protecting your data is crucial, and Windows 11 provides robust tools for file backup and recovery. Utilizing File History, you can automatically back up versions of your files to an external drive or network location. To set up File History, go to `Settings` > `Update & Security` > `Backup` and follow the instructions to choose a drive and start the backup process. In the event of data loss, you can restore files from your backup, providing peace of mind and ensuring that your important documents and memories are safeguarded.

Understanding File History: File History is a feature that continuously protects your files by copying them to an external drive or network location. Once activated, it will save copies of your files at intervals you can specify, allowing you to go back and retrieve earlier versions of a file if needed. This is especially useful for documents that undergo frequent changes, as you can revert to a previous version with ease. To manage File History settings, navigate to `Settings` > `Update & Security` > `Backup` and click on `More options`. Here, you can adjust how often backups are made and how long they are kept, tailoring the feature to your specific needs.

By embracing these advanced features of file management in Windows 11, seniors can ensure that their digital files are not only well-organized but also easily accessible, securely shared, and adequately backed up. These practices contribute to a more efficient and enjoyable computing experience, allowing users to focus more on their interests and less on the technicalities of file management.

Managing Files and Folders

For those who have amassed a significant collection of files and documents, the ability to **tag** and **search** using metadata becomes indispensable. This advanced functionality in Windows 11 allows for a more nuanced approach to file management. By right-clicking on a file and selecting `Properties`, you can navigate to the `Details` tab where you have the option to add or edit **tags** and **metadata**. This could include details such as the author for documents, or the date taken for photographs. This method of categorization is particularly useful for projects that span multiple file types and categories, enabling a multifaceted search capability beyond simple file names.

Furthermore, the **Quick Access** feature in File Explorer can dramatically streamline how you access frequently used files and folders. By pinning your most accessed locations to Quick Access, you're able to immediately navigate to these areas upon opening File Explorer, bypassing the need to traverse through your storage hierarchy. To pin a folder to Quick Access, right-click on it and select `Pin to Quick Access`. This is especially beneficial for those who work on long-term projects or frequently access specific documents.

File sharing has also been simplified in Windows 11, with several options available to suit different needs. For sharing within a home network, **Windows File Sharing** allows you to share documents, photos, and other files with computers on the same network. To share a file or folder, right-click it, select `Give access to`, and then choose `Specific people`. From here, you can select who on your network you wish to share with. For sharing outside of a home network, **OneDrive** offers a convenient solution. Right-click the file you wish to share, select `Share`, and then choose how you want to share the file, whether it be a link via email or directly through OneDrive.

Backing up your files is crucial, and Windows 11 provides **File History**, a tool that automatically backs up versions of your files to an external drive or network location. To enable File History, connect an external drive, go to `Settings` > `Update & Security` > `Backup`, and then select `Add a drive` to choose your external drive. Once File History is enabled, you can customize how often backups occur and how long they are kept by clicking on `More options` under the Backup section in Settings.

For those who need to access files across multiple devices, **OneDrive** is integrated directly into File Explorer, providing a seamless cloud storage solution. Files saved to OneDrive are accessible from any device with an internet connection, ensuring that your documents and photos are always at your fingertips. To manage your OneDrive storage, click on the OneDrive icon in the taskbar's notification area, where you can check your storage status and access OneDrive settings.

In managing large volumes of files, **keyboard shortcuts** can significantly enhance your efficiency. Familiarize yourself with shortcuts such as `Ctrl` + `C` for copy, `Ctrl` + `V` for paste, and `Ctrl` + `X` for cut. Additionally, `Ctrl` + `Z` can undo an action, while `Ctrl` + `Y` can redo it. These shortcuts, along with others like `Ctrl` + `A` to select all files in a folder, can save precious time and streamline your file management process.

Lastly, for those looking to maintain a tidy digital space, **cleaning up temporary files and unneeded downloads** can free up storage and improve system performance. Windows 11 includes a **Storage Sense** feature that can automatically delete temporary files and empty the Recycle Bin at intervals you specify. To configure Storage Sense, go to `Settings` > `System` > `Storage` and toggle on Storage Sense. From here, you can customize how it operates to best suit your needs, ensuring that your device remains clutter-free and operates efficiently.

Creating and Organizing Folders

Creating and organizing folders in Windows 11 is a cornerstone of effective digital file management, enabling users to maintain a clean and structured workspace. The process begins with a simple right-click in the desired location within File Explorer, followed by selecting New and then Folder. This action creates a new folder, which can be immediately named to reflect its intended contents. The naming convention should be intuitive, allowing for easy recall and access in the future. For example, a folder named Tax Documents 2025 clearly indicates its contents, facilitating quick navigation.

Beyond basic folder creation, the organization can be further refined through the use of subfolders, which can be created following the same steps. This hierarchical structure allows for granular categorization of files, akin to a digital filing cabinet. For instance, within the Tax Documents 2025 folder, subfolders named Receipts, Forms, and Correspondence can segregate documents by type, streamlining the retrieval process.

The utility of folders extends beyond mere organization; it also plays a critical role in data management strategies such as archiving and backup. By consolidating files of a similar nature or related to a specific project into a single folder, users can easily move or back up these collections to external drives or cloud storage solutions. This is particularly advantageous for ensuring data redundancy and facilitating recovery in the event of system failure or data loss.

For those managing extensive collections of files, Windows 11 offers advanced search capabilities that can be leveraged to locate folders quickly. By entering the folder name in the File Explorer search bar, the system can display matching results in real-time, reducing the need to manually navigate through directories. Additionally, the Quick Access feature in File Explorer can be utilized to pin frequently accessed folders, ensuring they are always readily available upon opening File Explorer.

When it comes to sharing files with others, organized folders simplify the process. Users can share an entire folder, rather than individual files, via OneDrive or other file-sharing platforms. This is particularly useful for collaborative projects, where multiple documents need to be accessed by various stakeholders. To share a folder, right-click it, select Share, and then choose the appropriate sharing method based on the recipient's access requirements.

In the realm of customization, Windows 11 allows users to modify folder views to suit their preferences. This can be achieved by navigating to the View tab in File Explorer, where options such as Details, List, Tiles, and Content can alter how files and folders are displayed. For those dealing with multimedia files, the Extra large icons view can be particularly useful, providing visual previews of image and video files.

Moreover, Windows 11 supports the tagging of files within folders, offering an additional layer of organization. By right-clicking a file, selecting Properties, and navigating to the Details tab, users can add tags to files, facilitating easier retrieval through search. This feature is invaluable for projects encompassing diverse file types and subjects, enabling users to filter and locate files based on custom tags.

In conclusion, mastering the creation and organization of folders in Windows 11 empowers users to maintain an efficient, orderly digital environment. By adopting a systematic approach to file management, individuals can enhance productivity, safeguard important documents, and enjoy a more streamlined computing experience.

Using OneDrive for Cloud Storage

OneDrive, Microsoft's integrated cloud storage solution, offers a seamless way to store, access, and share files across all your devices. With OneDrive, your documents, photos, and other important files are not just stored safely in the cloud but are also accessible from anywhere, on any device with internet access. This is particularly advantageous for seniors who may use multiple devices or who want the peace of mind that comes with having backups of their precious memories and important documents.

To begin using OneDrive on Windows 11, you'll first need to sign in with your Microsoft account. If you don't already have one, creating a Microsoft account is a straightforward process that can be completed for free. Once signed in, you'll find the OneDrive icon located in the system tray at the bottom right corner of your screen. Clicking this icon opens the OneDrive folder, which operates just like any other folder on your computer, with the added benefit of being synced to the cloud.

Uploading files to OneDrive is as simple as dragging and dropping them into the OneDrive folder or saving them directly to OneDrive from your favorite apps. For instance, when saving a document in Microsoft Word, you can choose OneDrive as the location, which automatically uploads the document to the cloud. This method ensures that your files are not only saved locally on your computer but are also backed up online.

Sharing files or folders with family and friends is another key feature of OneDrive. Right-click on the file or folder you wish to share, select `Share` from the context menu, and then choose how you want to share. You can send a link via email, get a link to copy and paste, or even set permissions for the file, deciding whether recipients can view or edit the content. This feature is particularly useful for sharing photos, documents, or even entire folders without the need for cumbersome email attachments.

Accessing files on different devices is a breeze with OneDrive. Whether you're on a tablet, smartphone, or another computer, as long as you're signed in with your Microsoft account, you can access your OneDrive files. This cross-device accessibility is especially beneficial for seniors who may not always be at their primary computer but need access to their files.

Managing storage space effectively is crucial, as the free version of OneDrive offers a limited amount of storage. However, additional storage can be purchased if needed. To manage your storage, regularly review your OneDrive files and delete those you no longer need. Also, take advantage of OneDrive's storage management settings, which can help optimize space by making files available on-demand rather than storing them locally on every device.

For those concerned about **privacy and security**, OneDrive provides robust measures to protect your data. Files stored in OneDrive are encrypted, both in transit and at rest, offering a high level of security against unauthorized access. Additionally, you can enhance the security of your OneDrive account by enabling two-factor authentication (2FA), adding an extra layer of protection beyond just your password.

In summary, OneDrive is an invaluable tool for seniors looking to store, share, and access their files with ease and security. Its integration into Windows 11 makes it an accessible and convenient option for anyone looking to leverage cloud storage. By familiarizing yourself with OneDrive's features and settings, you can take full advantage of this powerful tool to simplify your digital life.

Setting Up OneDrive

Once you have familiarized yourself with the basics of OneDrive and its integral role in cloud storage for Windows 11, the next step is to set up OneDrive to work seamlessly across all your devices. This process begins on your Windows 11 computer and extends to any other device you might use, including tablets and smartphones. The initial setup is a straightforward process that ensures your files are automatically backed up to the cloud and accessible wherever you go.

First, ensure that you are logged into your computer with a Microsoft account. This is a prerequisite for accessing OneDrive, as it ties all your files and settings across devices. If you have not yet signed in with a Microsoft account, you can do so through the **Settings** app under **Accounts**. Once signed in, you'll notice the OneDrive icon in the notification area at the bottom right corner of your screen, indicating that OneDrive is active.

To start the setup, click on the OneDrive icon. If this is your first time accessing OneDrive, a setup wizard will guide you through the process. The wizard will prompt you to sign in with your Microsoft account if you haven't already. After signing in, you'll be presented with the option to choose the location for your OneDrive folder. The default location is usually sufficient, but you have the flexibility to select a different location if your storage needs require it.

After selecting the folder location, the next step involves choosing which folders you want to sync from your PC to OneDrive. You don't have to sync everything; select the folders that contain files you wish to access across your devices or those you want to ensure are backed up. This selective sync feature helps manage your cloud storage space more efficiently, especially if you're using the free version of OneDrive with limited storage capacity.

Once the setup is complete, files saved to your OneDrive folder are automatically synced to the cloud. You can verify this by looking for the OneDrive icons on your files and folders. A green checkmark indicates that the file is synced and up to date, while a cloud icon means the file is available online only, helping you save space on your device.

For enhanced functionality, consider installing the OneDrive app on your other devices, such as your smartphone or tablet. The OneDrive app is available for both iOS and Android devices and can be downloaded from their respective app stores. Logging into the app with the same Microsoft account will give you access to all your synced files, allowing for a seamless workflow between your computer and mobile devices.

Remember, managing your files effectively in OneDrive involves regular maintenance. Periodically review your files and folders, deleting those you no longer need and organizing the rest into clearly named folders. This not only helps keep your cloud storage tidy but also makes it easier to find and access your files when you need them.

Additionally, take advantage of OneDrive's online features by logging into the OneDrive website. Here, you can share files or folders directly from the web, view photos, and even edit Microsoft Office documents in your browser without needing to install the Office apps on your computer. This web functionality extends the versatility of OneDrive, making it a powerful tool for not just storage but also for collaboration and productivity.

By following these steps to set up and manage OneDrive, you harness the full potential of cloud storage, ensuring your files are safe, secure, and accessible no matter where you are. With OneDrive integrated into Windows 11, embracing the cloud becomes a natural extension of your computer's file system, simplifying your digital life and providing peace of mind that your data is always backed up and within reach.

Sharing Files and Folders

Sharing files and folders through OneDrive not only simplifies collaboration but also enhances the flexibility of accessing shared content across multiple devices. When you share a file or folder from OneDrive, you have the option to control the level of access others have, ranging from view-only to full edit capabilities. This granular control is crucial for maintaining the integrity of your documents while facilitating productive collaboration. To share a document, right-click on the file or folder within your OneDrive directory, select Share, and then choose the appropriate sharing options. You can specify whether recipients can edit or only view the files, which is particularly useful when disseminating information that should not be altered.

For instances where collaboration is key, such as working on a family event planning document or a community newsletter, OneDrive allows you to invite others to collaborate in real-time. This is achieved by sending an invite via email directly from the OneDrive interface. The recipients receive a link that opens the document in their web browser, allowing for immediate collaboration. This feature is supported by the integration of Microsoft Office Online, enabling you and your collaborators to edit documents, spreadsheets, and presentations simultaneously, seeing each other's changes in real-time.

Moreover, OneDrive offers an advanced sharing feature known as link expiration. This feature is particularly useful for sharing files or folders temporarily. By setting an expiration date on the share link, you ensure that access to the content is automatically revoked after a certain period, enhancing the security of your shared data. To use this feature, when you create a share link, select More options and then set an expiration date for the link. This method is ideal for sharing sensitive information that should not be accessible indefinitely.

Another layer of security when sharing files and folders is the ability to set passwords for shared links. This means that even if the link is forwarded or falls into the wrong hands, only those with the password can access the content. To apply a password, in the Share dialog box, choose More options and then select Set password. Enter a strong, unique password and communicate it to your intended recipients through a secure channel.

For those who frequently share content with the same group of people, OneDrive allows the creation of shared libraries. These libraries are essentially shared folders where members can store, access, and collaborate on files. This is particularly advantageous for ongoing projects or family archives where multiple people need regular access. To create a shared library, navigate to your OneDrive on the web, select Create shared library, and then follow the prompts to set it up and invite members.

In the realm of file management and sharing, it's also important to understand how to manage shared content. OneDrive provides a comprehensive Shared view, accessible both from the desktop app and online, which displays all the files and folders you've shared with others as well as those shared with you. This centralized view makes it easy to monitor who has access to what and to revoke access if necessary. To manage permissions or stop sharing, simply find the file or folder in question under the Shared view, select it, and then choose Manage access. From here, you can modify permissions or remove access entirely.

Lastly, for those concerned about accidentally deleting shared files, OneDrive offers version history for documents. This feature allows you to restore previous versions of your files, safeguarding against accidental deletions or unwanted edits. To access version history, right-click on the file in OneDrive and select Version history. You can then view and restore previous versions as needed.

By leveraging these sharing and collaboration features of OneDrive, you can enhance your productivity and ensure that your files are shared securely and efficiently. Whether you're collaborating on a project, sharing family photos, or distributing community newsletters, OneDrive's sharing capabilities are designed to meet a wide range of needs while providing the control and security necessary for peace of mind.

Protecting Your Data

Protecting your data on Windows 11 involves a multifaceted approach that encompasses both local and cloud-based strategies to ensure your information remains secure and recoverable in the event of a mishap. One critical aspect of data protection is **regularly backing up your files**. Windows 11 includes a built-in feature known as **File History**, which, once activated, automatically backs up copies of your files to an external drive or network location. To set up File History, connect an external storage device to your computer, then navigate to `Settings` > `Update & Security` > `Backup`. Click `Add a drive` and select your external drive. With File History enabled, you can customize how often backups occur and how long versions are kept.

Another layer of protection is provided by **Windows Defender**, a comprehensive security tool that offers real-time protection against viruses, malware, and ransomware. It's vital to ensure that Windows Defender is always updated to safeguard your data from the latest threats. You can check the status of Windows Defender by going to `Settings` > `Update & Security` > `Windows Security`.

For sensitive information, **BitLocker** offers an additional level of security. BitLocker is a full disk encryption feature included with Windows 11, designed to protect data by encrypting the entire drive that Windows is installed on. If your device is lost or stolen, BitLocker ensures that your data is inaccessible without the correct password or recovery key. To enable BitLocker, search for `BitLocker` in the Start menu and follow the instructions to encrypt your drive.

Using strong passwords and changing them regularly is another fundamental practice for protecting your data. Ensure that your Microsoft account, which is tied to OneDrive and your Windows login, has a robust password. Consider using a password manager to generate and store complex passwords for various accounts.

In addition to these measures, be cautious of **phishing attacks** and **malware**. Do not click on suspicious links in emails or download attachments from unknown sources. Always ensure that your software, especially your web browser and operating system, is up to date with the latest security patches.

For those who prefer cloud storage, **OneDrive offers Personal Vault**, a protected area within OneDrive designed for sensitive information. Files in Personal Vault require two-factor authentication (2FA) to access, adding an extra layer of security. To use Personal Vault, open your OneDrive folder and select `Personal Vault`. Follow the prompts to set it up and begin adding files.

Lastly, consider **encrypting your email communications** when sending sensitive information. Windows 11 supports email encryption through Outlook. To send an encrypted email, compose your message in Outlook, click on `Options`, then `Encrypt`, and choose the encryption option that suits your needs.

By implementing these strategies, you can significantly enhance the protection of your data on Windows 11. Regularly review your security settings and practices to ensure that your information remains safe from emerging threats.

Backup and Recovery Options

Beyond the foundational practices of file management and leveraging cloud storage solutions like OneDrive, a comprehensive approach to safeguarding your data on Windows 11 involves exploring the built-in backup and recovery options that Microsoft has thoughtfully integrated into the operating system. These tools are designed not only to protect against data loss but also to provide a straightforward path to recovery should you encounter system failures or other unforeseen issues that could compromise your files.

The cornerstone of Windows 11's backup capabilities is the **File History** feature, which allows for automatic backups of your personal files to an external drive or network location. To activate File History, you would navigate to `Settings` > `Update & Security` > `Backup`, then click on `Add a drive` and select an external drive as your backup destination. Once File History is enabled, it's crucial to customize its settings to fit your specific needs, such as determining how frequently backups should occur and the duration for which backup versions are retained. This customization ensures that your data protection strategy aligns with your usage patterns and storage capacity, offering peace of mind that your files are securely backed up without unnecessarily consuming space.

In addition to File History, Windows 11 includes a feature known as **System Image Backup**, which creates a complete snapshot of your system at a specific point in time. This snapshot includes not only your personal files but also the operating system, installed programs, and system settings. To create a system image, you would access the Control Panel, navigate to `System and Security` > `Backup and Restore (Windows 7)`, and then select `Create a system image`. Opting to store this image on an external hard drive or network location ensures that you have a comprehensive backup that can be used to restore your entire system to its previous state in the event of a critical failure. It's advisable to create system images periodically, especially before making significant changes to your system or installing new hardware, to facilitate a smooth recovery process if needed.

For those instances where your system encounters an issue that prevents it from starting properly, Windows 11 provides **Advanced Startup Options**, including the ability to boot from a recovery drive. Creating a recovery drive is a proactive measure that involves using a USB flash drive to store a copy of Windows 11's recovery environment. This can be accomplished by searching for `Create a recovery drive` in the Start menu and following the on-screen instructions. With a recovery drive at your disposal, you can boot your computer from the USB drive to access diagnostic tools and recovery options, such as `Reset this PC`, `System Restore`, and `Command Prompt` for advanced troubleshooting. This capability is invaluable for addressing startup issues, repairing system files, and performing system restores without requiring access to the operating system's normal boot sequence.

Furthermore, the integration of **OneDrive's Personal Vault** offers an additional layer of security for your most sensitive information. By utilizing Personal Vault's two-factor authentication requirement for access, you ensure that even if your physical device is compromised, the data stored within Personal Vault remains protected against unauthorized access. Regularly moving important files to Personal Vault and ensuring that your OneDrive account utilizes strong, unique passwords and, where possible, two-factor authentication, enhances the overall security of your digital life.

It's also worth noting the importance of staying informed about the latest updates and security patches released by Microsoft. Ensuring that your system is always up to date is a critical component of a robust data protection strategy. Windows 11 is designed to automatically download and install updates by default, but manually verifying that your system is up to date can help prevent vulnerabilities that could be exploited to compromise your data.

Understanding File History

File History is a vital component of Windows 11 designed to protect your data by automatically backing up versions of your files in the Documents, Music, Pictures, Videos, and Desktop folders. If you ever lose a file or need to revert to an earlier version, File History makes it possible without requiring extensive technical knowledge. To activate File History, you first need an external drive or network location where backups will be stored. Connect your external drive to your computer, then navigate to `Settings > Update & Security > Backup`. Here, you'll find the option to `Add a drive` under the `Back up using File History` section. Select your external drive from the list, and Windows will set it as your backup drive.

After setting up your drive, you can further customize File History's settings by clicking on `More options`. Here, you can adjust how often backups are made, ranging from every 10 minutes to daily, and set how long versions are kept, from until space is needed to forever. It's also possible to add folders to the backup or exclude certain folders if you prefer not to back them up. For those with a keen interest in maintaining a streamlined backup process, these options provide a level of control that ensures only necessary data is preserved, thus optimizing storage space.

In the event you need to restore files from a backup, navigate back to the `Backup` settings and click on `More options`. Scroll down to the bottom of the page and select `Restore files from a current backup`. This action opens the File History restore tool, which displays files and folders in a timeline view. You can navigate through different versions of your files by date, and once you find the version you wish to restore, simply select it and click the `Restore` button to bring it back to its original location. If the original location is no longer available or you prefer to restore the file to a different location, right-click the `Restore` button and choose `Restore to`, then select a new destination.

File History is not just a backup tool; it's a robust system designed to give users peace of mind, knowing their valuable data is protected against accidental deletion or corruption. By leveraging this feature, seniors can ensure their digital memories and important documents are safely archived, with the flexibility to access previous versions at any time. It's a testament to Windows 11's commitment to accessibility and user-friendly design, allowing individuals of all tech-savviness levels to secure their digital life with minimal effort.

Chapter 5: Security and Maintenance

Ensuring the security of your Windows 11 system is paramount, especially in an era where digital threats are increasingly sophisticated. **Windows Security Essentials** provides a comprehensive suite of tools designed to protect your computer from viruses, malware, and other security threats. This integrated feature automatically scans your system for malicious software and offers real-time protection, ensuring that your data remains safe from unauthorized access. To access Windows Security Essentials, simply navigate to `Settings > Update & Security > Windows Security`. Here, you'll find various options to review your device's security status and take action on any identified risks.

Another critical aspect of maintaining a secure Windows 11 environment is the **setting up of firewalls and parental controls**. Firewalls act as a barrier between your computer and the internet, blocking unauthorized access while permitting outward communication. This is crucial for preventing potential hackers from accessing your personal information. To configure your firewall settings, go to `Control Panel > System and Security > Windows Defender Firewall`. From here, you can adjust your firewall settings to meet your specific security needs.

Parental controls are an essential feature for users who wish to manage the content accessible on their computer, making it a safe environment for all family members. Windows 11 allows you to set up accounts with customizable restrictions for each user, controlling their access to applications, games, and websites, and even setting time limits on computer use. To set up parental controls, navigate to `Settings > Accounts > Family & other users` and follow the prompts to add a family member and customize their access levels.

As we delve deeper into the realm of security and maintenance, it's important to remember that staying informed about the latest security updates and practices is key to safeguarding your digital life. Windows 11 is designed with security at its core, offering tools and features that empower users to maintain a high level of protection against evolving digital threats.

Regularly checking for Windows updates is another fundamental step in ensuring your system's security and optimal performance. Microsoft frequently releases updates that include not only new features but also critical security patches to protect against newly discovered vulnerabilities. To manually check for updates, go to `Settings > Update & Security > Windows Update` and select `Check for updates`. If updates are available, it's advisable to install them as soon as possible to keep your system secure and functioning smoothly.

Optimizing your computer's performance can also contribute significantly to its maintenance and longevity. Over time, files and applications can accumulate, potentially slowing down your system. Utilizing built-in tools like Disk Cleanup and Storage Sense can help free up space and improve performance. Disk Cleanup can be accessed by searching for it in the Start menu, allowing you to remove temporary files, system files, and even previous Windows installations that are no longer necessary. Storage Sense, found in `Settings > System > Storage`, automates this process, offering options to automatically delete unnecessary files and manage how content is stored on your device.

Troubleshooting common issues is an integral part of maintaining a healthy Windows 11 system. For internet connectivity problems, running the Network Troubleshooter can help diagnose and solve many common network issues. This tool can be accessed by going to `Settings > Network & Internet > Status` and selecting `Network troubleshooter`. For printer and device issues, ensuring that your drivers are up to date is crucial. Drivers can be updated through the Device Manager, which is accessible by right-clicking the Start button and selecting `Device Manager`. From there, you can see if any devices have a yellow exclamation mark indicating a problem and update drivers by right-clicking on the device and selecting `Update driver`.

By adopting these practices, seniors can confidently navigate the complexities of Windows 11, ensuring their systems are secure, optimized, and maintained. Leveraging the built-in features and tools provided by Windows 11 not only enhances the user experience but also contributes to a safer and more reliable computing environment. Remember, maintaining your computer is an ongoing process that requires regular attention to ensure it continues to serve your needs effectively and securely.

Keeping Windows 11 Secure

Ensuring the **security** of your Windows 11 system extends beyond the initial setup of **Windows Security Essentials**, **firewalls**, and **parental controls**. It involves a proactive approach to safeguarding your personal information and maintaining the integrity of your computer's operations. **Regularly updating your software** is crucial in this regard. Microsoft, along with other software developers, frequently releases updates that not only introduce new features but also patch security vulnerabilities. To manually update your software, navigate to `Settings > Update & Security > Windows Update` and click on `Check for updates`. If updates are available, follow the prompts to install them, thereby ensuring your system is protected against the latest threats.

Creating strong passwords and managing them effectively is another cornerstone of digital security. Utilize a password manager to generate and store complex passwords. This tool can significantly enhance your online security by creating unique, strong passwords for each of your accounts, which are then encrypted and accessible through a master password. Remember, using the same password across multiple sites increases your vulnerability to cyber attacks.

Activating two-factor authentication (2FA) wherever possible adds an extra layer of security to your accounts. This method requires not only your password but also a second piece of information—usually a code sent to your phone or generated by an app—before granting access to your account. To set up 2FA, visit the security settings of your online accounts and follow the provided instructions.

Being vigilant about phishing attempts is essential. Phishing emails and messages attempt to trick you into revealing sensitive information by impersonating legitimate companies or contacts. Always verify the sender's email address, and avoid clicking on links or downloading attachments from unknown or suspicious sources. Instead, go directly to the website by typing the URL into your browser.

Using a Virtual Private Network (VPN) can significantly increase your privacy online, especially when connected to public Wi-Fi networks. A VPN encrypts your internet connection, making it difficult for hackers to intercept and steal your data. There are many reputable VPN services available; choose one that fits your needs and budget.

Backing up your data regularly is a critical practice that cannot be overstated. Use Windows 11's built-in tools like **File History** or a cloud storage service to create copies of your important files. This ensures that in the event of a hardware failure, ransomware attack, or other data loss scenarios, you can restore your information from the backup. To set up File History, connect an external drive, then navigate to `Settings > Update & Security > Backup`, and follow the prompts to select your drive and configure your backup settings.

Educating yourself about the latest cybersecurity threats and staying informed about how to protect against them is invaluable. Cyber threats evolve rapidly, and being aware of the latest scams, vulnerabilities, and protection strategies is key to maintaining a secure system.

By implementing these practices, you can significantly enhance the security of your Windows 11 system and protect your digital life. Remember, security is not a one-time setup but a continuous process of monitoring, updating, and adjusting your practices to counter new threats as they arise.

Windows Security Essentials

The **Windows Security Essentials** suite is an integral part of maintaining a robust defense against the myriad of digital threats that users face today. It encompasses a range of tools and features that are designed to detect, prevent, and remove malicious software while safeguarding your personal information. One of the key components of this suite is the **Virus & Threat Protection**. This feature continuously scans your computer for malware, viruses, ransomware, and other threats. Users can perform quick scans, full scans, or custom scans on specific folders or files by navigating to `Settings > Update & Security > Windows Security` and selecting `Virus & threat protection`. It's advisable to schedule regular scans to ensure ongoing protection.

Another vital aspect is the **Account Protection** feature, which helps secure your identity and information. It prompts you to set up dynamic lock, Windows Hello, and other sign-in options, enhancing security and making it more difficult for unauthorized users to gain access to your device. To access these options, go to the same Windows Security panel and select `Account protection`.

Firewall & Network Protection plays a crucial role in safeguarding your computer against unauthorized access through the internet or other networks. It monitors incoming and outgoing network traffic and allows you to set rules that determine which traffic is allowed or blocked. Users can adjust their firewall settings by navigating to `Control Panel > System and Security > Windows Defender Firewall`. Here, you can turn the firewall on or off and configure various settings to suit your security needs.

App & Browser Control in Windows Security provides an additional layer of protection by monitoring apps and files from the web, helping to prevent malicious software installations and untrusted applications from running. This feature can be particularly useful for seniors who might inadvertently download potentially harmful software. Access this feature through `Settings > Update & Security > Windows Security > App & browser control` to adjust the settings according to your preferences.

Device Security is another cornerstone of Windows Security Essentials, offering core isolation and memory integrity features that help protect the core parts of your Windows 11 system. This is especially important for preventing sophisticated attacks that target the system's core processes. To explore these options, select `Device security` from the Windows Security menu.

For comprehensive internet safety, the **Device Performance & Health** section provides an overview of your device's health, including storage capacity, battery life, and apps and software that might affect your device's performance. Regularly checking this section can help identify and resolve issues before they become problematic. Access it via `Settings > Update & Security > Windows Security > Device performance & health`.

Implementing these security measures requires a proactive approach. Regularly updating your Windows 11 system is critical, as updates often include patches for security vulnerabilities that have been discovered since the last update. To manually check for updates, go to `Settings > Update & Security > Windows Update` and click `Check for updates`.

Moreover, understanding the importance of **creating strong passwords, activating two-factor authentication**, and **being vigilant about phishing attempts** cannot be overstated. These practices are fundamental to securing your online presence and protecting your personal information from unauthorized access.

Utilizing a **Virtual Private Network (VPN)** and **regularly backing up your data** are also prudent measures. A VPN enhances your privacy online, especially on public Wi-Fi networks, by encrypting your internet connection. Regular data backups, whether through **File History** or a cloud storage service, ensure that you can recover your important files in the event of data loss.

In essence, leveraging the full spectrum of **Windows Security Essentials** tools and features, along with adopting safe computing practices, empowers seniors to navigate the digital world securely. These measures not only protect against current threats but also provide a foundation for adapting to future security challenges.

Firewalls and Parental Controls

Firewalls serve as the first line of defense in securing your Windows 11 system from unauthorized access. They meticulously monitor incoming and outgoing network traffic, applying rules that block potentially harmful communications without hindering your legitimate online activities. To tailor these settings to your specific needs, access the firewall configurations by entering `Control Panel > System and Security > Windows Defender Firewall` in the search bar. Here, you have the flexibility to turn the firewall on or off—though it's strongly advised to keep it always activated for optimal protection. Additionally, you can customize the settings to define exceptions for apps that you trust, ensuring they operate without unnecessary restrictions. This customization is crucial for applications that require internet access for updates or online functionality, allowing them to function seamlessly while maintaining the integrity of your system's security.

Parental controls in Windows 11 are designed with the safety of younger users in mind, offering a comprehensive suite of tools that empower you to create a secure and appropriate computing environment. By navigating to `Settings > Accounts > Family & other users`, you can add family members and configure their accounts with suitable limitations. This includes managing screen time, filtering content, and setting purchase limits, among other controls. For instance, you can restrict access to mature content on websites, ensuring that children are exposed only to age-appropriate material. Moreover, the activity reporting feature provides insights into the digital habits of your family members, allowing you to guide them towards healthier practices. Setting up these controls requires a Microsoft account, which facilitates the management of settings across multiple devices, ensuring a consistent protective environment regardless of the device being used.

Implementing firewalls and parental controls is a proactive step towards safeguarding your digital life and that of your family. While firewalls protect against external threats, parental controls help in creating a safe digital space for children, striking a balance between security and usability. It's important to regularly review and adjust these settings as your needs and the digital landscape evolve. Keeping abreast of the latest developments in cybersecurity can further enhance your protective measures, ensuring that your Windows 11 system remains a secure stronghold against both current and emerging threats. Engaging with these security features not only fortifies your system but also educates younger users about the importance of digital safety, fostering a culture of security awareness within the household.

System Maintenance and Updates

Maintaining your Windows 11 system involves a series of steps that ensure its smooth operation and longevity. A critical aspect of this maintenance is **regularly updating your operating system**. Microsoft releases updates that not only introduce new features but also address security vulnerabilities and software bugs. To manually check for updates, navigate to `Settings > Update & Security > Windows Update` and click on `Check for updates`. It's essential to install these updates promptly to protect your system from potential threats and improve its performance.

Another key component of system maintenance is **disk cleanup**. Over time, your computer accumulates unnecessary files that can take up valuable disk space and slow down performance. To access the Disk Cleanup tool, search for it in the Start menu, and select the drive you want to clean up. This tool allows you to delete temporary files, system files, and empty the Recycle Bin, freeing up space on your hard drive.

Defragmenting your hard drive is also beneficial, especially if you're using a traditional spinning hard drive. Defragmentation reorganizes the data on your hard drive, allowing for faster access and improved efficiency. To defragment your drive, search for 'Defragment and Optimize Drives' in the Start menu. Select your drive and click on `Optimize`. It's worth noting that if you're using an SSD (Solid State Drive), defragmentation is not necessary and is, in fact, not recommended as it can reduce the lifespan of the SSD.

Monitoring system health is another vital practice. Windows 11 includes a feature called **Windows Security**, which provides real-time protection against malware and other threats. To check your system's health, navigate to `Settings > Update & Security > Windows Security`. Here, you can view the health report, which includes details on virus and threat protection, firewall and network protection, app and browser control, device security, and device performance and health. Regularly reviewing this report can help you identify and resolve potential issues before they become serious problems.

Creating system restore points can be a lifesaver in case of system failure or other issues. Restore points allow you to revert your computer's system files and settings to an earlier point in time, without affecting personal files. To create a restore point, search for 'Create a restore point' in the Start menu, select your system drive, and click on `Create`. It's a good practice to create restore points before making significant changes to your system, such as installing new software or drivers.

Lastly, **backing up your data** is an essential part of system maintenance. Windows 11 offers built-in tools for backing up files, such as **File History** for backing up personal files and **System Image Backup** for creating a complete backup of your system. To set up File History, connect an external drive or select a network location, then navigate to `Settings > Update & Security > Backup` and follow the prompts. For System Image Backup, search for 'Backup settings' in the Start menu and follow the instructions under 'Looking for an older backup?'

By following these maintenance practices, you can ensure that your Windows 11 system remains secure, efficient, and reliable. Regular updates, disk cleanup, system monitoring, and data backup are all critical components of a comprehensive maintenance strategy. These steps not only enhance your computer's performance but also protect your data and ensure that your system can recover from unexpected issues.

Checking for Windows Updates

Ensuring your Windows 11 system remains up-to-date is pivotal for both security and performance. Microsoft frequently releases updates that not only patch vulnerabilities but also introduce new features and improvements. To manually check for updates, press the **Windows key**, type `Settings`, and press **Enter**. In the Settings window, navigate to **Update & Security**, a section dedicated to Windows Updates, security settings, and backup options. Here, you'll find the **Windows Update** tab on the sidebar. Clicking on it reveals the **Check for updates** button. When selected, Windows 11 will connect to Microsoft's servers to see if any updates are available for your system.

If updates are found, they will be listed, and you'll have the option to install them immediately or schedule them for later. It's advisable to install these updates as soon as possible to ensure your system's integrity. For major updates, Windows might need to restart. You can choose a convenient time for this to happen, preventing any disruption in your work or leisure activities.

Windows 11 also offers options for **Active Hours**, a feature that lets you specify the hours during which you're most likely to use your computer. Windows will avoid restarting your computer for updates during these hours, minimizing any inconvenience. To adjust Active Hours, go back to the **Windows Update** settings and look for the **Change active hours** option.

For those who prefer an even more hands-off approach, **Advanced options** under the same section provide further control over how updates are installed. Here, you can enable **Update notifications**, which inform you when a restart is required to complete an update installation. Additionally, you can select **Download updates over metered connections** if you're on a limited data plan, though this is not recommended unless necessary, as it could lead to additional charges from your internet service provider.

Remember, keeping your system updated is not just about having the latest features; it's a critical component of your digital security strategy. Regular updates ensure that vulnerabilities are patched, reducing the risk of malware or hacker exploitation. Therefore, make checking for and installing Windows updates a regular part of your computer maintenance routine.

Optimizing Performance

Beyond ensuring your system's security through regular updates, optimizing performance is crucial for a seamless Windows 11 experience. Over time, computers can accumulate unnecessary files and data, potentially slowing down performance. Leveraging built-in tools like **Disk Cleanup** and **Storage Sense** can significantly enhance your computer's efficiency. Disk Cleanup scans and removes temporary files, system files, and various types of unnecessary data that clutter your hard drive. To access Disk Cleanup, simply search for it in the Start menu, select the drive you wish to clean, and check the categories of files you're comfortable deleting.

Storage Sense, on the other hand, automates this process, working in the background to free up space by cleaning temporary files and content from your Recycle Bin. To configure Storage Sense, navigate to Settings > System > Storage and toggle on **Storage Sense**. You can customize how often Storage Sense runs, decide when to delete files in your Recycle Bin, and even manage how long to keep files in your Downloads folder before they're considered for deletion.

Another aspect of performance optimization involves managing the programs that run at startup. Some applications are programmed to start automatically when you log in, which can significantly slow down the startup process. To manage these, press Ctrl + Shift + Esc to open the Task Manager, then click on the **Startup** tab. Here, you'll see a list of applications with their impact on startup. Disabling non-essential applications can reduce startup times and free up resources.

Updating drivers is also key to maintaining optimal performance. Drivers are the software components that allow your operating system to communicate with hardware devices. Outdated drivers can cause devices to malfunction or not perform at their best. To update drivers, open **Device Manager** by right-clicking the Start button and selecting it from the menu. In Device Manager, right-click on a device and select **Update driver**. Choose **Search automatically for updated driver software** to let Windows find and install the latest driver.

Lastly, optimizing your computer's performance isn't just about what you can remove or update; it's also about monitoring and managing your resources effectively. The **Performance Monitor** tool in Windows 11 provides detailed system data, offering insights into how your computer's hardware and software are performing. To access it, simply type Performance Monitor into the Start menu search and select it. This tool can help you identify bottlenecks and areas that may need attention, whether it's upgrading hardware or tweaking settings for better performance.

By taking proactive steps to manage your system's resources, you can ensure that your Windows 11 computer remains fast, responsive, and capable of handling whatever tasks you may need, from everyday computing to more demanding applications.

Troubleshooting Common Issues

When encountering **Internet Connectivity Problems**, the first step is to run the **Network Troubleshooter**. This built-in tool automatically diagnoses and fixes common network issues. Access it by right-clicking the network icon in the taskbar, selecting **Troubleshoot problems**, and following the on-screen instructions. If the troubleshooter doesn't resolve the issue, check if other devices on your network can connect to the internet. If they cannot, the problem might lie with your modem or router. Restarting these devices can often resolve connectivity issues. Unplug them, wait for about a minute, and then plug them back in. Wait for the devices to fully restart and try connecting again.

For **Solving Printer and Device Issues**, Windows 11 includes the **Device Manager**, a central location for managing hardware devices. To access it, right-click the Start button and select **Device Manager**. If your printer or another device isn't working correctly, locate it in the Device Manager list, right-click it, and select **Update driver**. Choose

Search automatically for updated driver software to allow Windows to find and install the latest drivers. If an update doesn't solve the problem, right-click the device again, this time selecting **Uninstall device**. Restart your computer after uninstalling, and Windows should automatically reinstall the device with the correct drivers.

Another common issue is when an application or program **fails to respond or crashes**. If this happens, use the **Task Manager** to end the task safely. Press Ctrl + Shift + Esc to open Task Manager, find the unresponsive program in the list, select it, and click **End Task**. This should close the program, allowing you to reopen it and try again. If the problem persists, check for updates for the application or consider reinstalling it.

Blue Screen Errors, also known as **Blue Screen of Death (BSOD)**, can be more daunting. They usually occur due to hardware or driver issues. When you encounter a BSOD, Windows will often restart automatically and attempt to resolve the issue. If you frequently encounter BSODs, note down the error code provided on the screen. You can search this code online or use it when seeking technical support to identify and solve the underlying problem. Additionally, ensuring all your drivers are up to date and running a system file check (sfc /scannow in Command Prompt) can help prevent these errors.

Lastly, if you're facing **slow system performance**, consider running the **Disk Cleanup** tool to remove temporary files and system files that may be cluttering your hard drive and affecting performance. Access Disk Cleanup by searching for it in the Start menu, selecting the drive you want to clean, and choosing the file types to delete. Following this, check the **Startup** tab in Task Manager to disable any unnecessary programs that run on startup, potentially slowing down your computer.

Remember, while troubleshooting, patience and a step-by-step approach are key. Often, simple solutions like restarting your device or checking for updates can resolve common issues. For more persistent problems, Windows 11 provides a range of tools and utilities designed to diagnose and fix issues, ensuring your computing experience remains smooth and efficient.

Internet Connectivity Problems

Continuing from the initial steps of troubleshooting internet connectivity issues, it's essential to delve deeper into the settings and configurations that can impact your online experience. After ensuring that the problem isn't with the modem or router and that other devices are also unable to connect, the next step involves examining the network settings on your Windows 11 computer.

One critical area to investigate is the IP configuration. Sometimes, the issue might stem from an incorrect IP address or DNS server settings. To check this, open Command Prompt by typing `cmd` in the Start menu search bar. Once opened, type `ipconfig /all` and press Enter. This command displays all your network connection details. Look for the `IPv4 Address` and `DNS Servers` entries. If the IPv4 address starts with `169.254`, it indicates that your computer is having trouble obtaining an IP address from the router. In such cases, releasing and renewing the IP address can sometimes resolve the issue. To do this, type `ipconfig /release` followed by `ipconfig /renew` in the Command Prompt.

If the problem persists, checking the DNS settings is another crucial step. A misconfigured DNS can lead to connection problems. To modify DNS settings, navigate to `Settings > Network & Internet > Wi-Fi` (or `Ethernet` if you're using a wired connection) and select your network. Scroll down to `IP settings` and click `Edit` under `DNS settings`. Switch the setting to `Manual`, and under `Preferred DNS`, you can enter `8.8.8.8` (Google's DNS server) or `1.1.1.1` (Cloudflare's DNS server) for a more reliable DNS resolution.

Another potential culprit could be Windows Firewall, which might inadvertently block certain internet connections. To ensure this isn't the case, type `Windows Security` in the Start menu search bar and select the app. Navigate to `Firewall & network protection`, click on your active network, and ensure that the Windows Defender Firewall is not blocking the connection. If you're unsure, temporarily disable the firewall to see if the connectivity issues resolve. Remember, it's crucial to re-enable the firewall immediately after testing to keep your system secure.

For users experiencing connectivity issues with Wi-Fi, forgetting the network and reconnecting can sometimes fix the problem. Go to `Settings > Network & Internet > Wi-Fi`, click on `Manage known networks`, select the problematic network, and click `Forget`. Afterward, reconnect to the network by entering the password again.

Lastly, if you've exhausted all other options, resetting the network settings might be necessary. This action will remove all network adapters and set everything back to the original configuration, potentially resolving any lingering issues. To reset your network, navigate to `Settings > Network & Internet > Advanced network settings` and click on `Network reset`. Confirm the action and restart your computer to apply the changes.

Solving Printer and Device Issues

When addressing printer and device issues on Windows 11, it's essential to delve into the **Device Manager** for a comprehensive overview of hardware functionality and driver status. This tool is instrumental in identifying devices that are malfunctioning or have outdated drivers, which can often be the root cause of connectivity problems or suboptimal performance. To access the **Device Manager**, right-click the Start button and select it from the context menu. Within this interface, you'll find a list of all the hardware components connected to your computer. Devices with issues are typically marked with a yellow exclamation point, indicating a problem that needs your attention.

For printers specifically, ensuring that they are properly connected and recognized by Windows 11 is the first step in troubleshooting. If your printer is connected via USB, try disconnecting and then reconnecting the cable to both the printer and the computer. For wireless printers, ensure that the printer is connected to the same Wi-Fi network as your computer. Sometimes, simply turning the printer off and on again can re-establish communication between the device and your PC.

If connectivity isn't the issue, the next step is to check for driver updates. In the **Device Manager**, locate your printer, right-click on it, and select **Update driver**. Opt for **Search automatically for updated driver software** to allow Windows to search the internet and your computer for the latest driver software. If an update is found, follow the prompts to install it. This process can resolve many issues related to printer functionality.

In cases where updating the driver doesn't solve the problem, you might need to uninstall and then reinstall the printer. Right-click on the printer in the **Device Manager** and select **Uninstall device**. After uninstallation, reboot your computer. Upon restart, Windows 11 should automatically detect the printer and attempt to reinstall it. If this doesn't happen, you may need to manually add the printer by going to `Settings > Devices > Printers & scanners` and selecting **Add a printer or scanner**. Windows will then guide you through the process of installing the printer.

Another critical aspect of solving printer and device issues is ensuring that the **Print Spooler** service is running smoothly. The Print Spooler manages print jobs sent to the printer, and if it's not functioning correctly, it can prevent documents from being printed. To check the status of the Print Spooler, press `Windows key + R` to open the Run dialog, type `services.msc`, and press **Enter**. In the Services window, scroll down to find the **Print Spooler** service. If it's not running, right-click it and select **Start**. If it is running but you're still experiencing issues, try restarting the service by right-clicking it, selecting **Restart**, and then attempting to print again.

For devices other than printers, similar principles apply. Ensuring that they are properly connected, checking for driver updates, and, if necessary, uninstalling and reinstalling the device can often resolve issues. For external devices like USB drives, cameras, or external hard drives, checking different USB ports can also be a simple but effective troubleshooting step. Sometimes, ports can malfunction or provide insufficient power, leading to connectivity issues.

Moreover, leveraging the **Troubleshoot** feature in Windows 11 can provide additional insights into resolving printer and device issues. To access it, go to `Settings > Update & Security > Troubleshoot > Additional troubleshooters`. Here, you'll find various troubleshooters for different types of issues, including one specifically for printers. Running the printer troubleshooter can help identify and automatically fix some common problems related to printer connectivity and functionality.

By methodically working through these steps, most printer and device issues on Windows 11 can be effectively resolved. However, if problems persist, it may be necessary to consult the device manufacturer's support website for more specific guidance or consider seeking professional technical assistance. Remember, maintaining up-to-date drivers and regularly checking device connections can prevent many common issues from arising, ensuring a smoother and more reliable experience with Windows 11.

Chapter 6: Advanced Features & Customization

Maximizing the utility of **Virtual Desktops** and **Task View** in Windows 11 can significantly enhance productivity and organization, especially for users who manage multiple projects or prefer to compartmentalize their digital workspace. **Virtual Desktops** allow you to create separate desktops for different purposes. For instance, one desktop could be dedicated to personal use, featuring apps like Photos and Spotify, while another could be set up for work, with quick access to Microsoft Office apps and your email client. To create a new virtual desktop, press `Win + Ctrl + D`. Switching between desktops is just as straightforward; use `Win + Ctrl + Left Arrow` or `Win + Ctrl + Right Arrow` to navigate through your open desktops. This feature is particularly useful for seniors who might be working on different hobbies or projects and wish to keep their resources organized and easily accessible.

Task View, accessed by pressing `Win + Tab`, provides an overview of all open windows and virtual desktops. It's an efficient way to manage your workspace, allowing you to move applications between desktops. This can be done by dragging and dropping windows into the desired desktop at the bottom of the screen. For those who prefer a clutter-free digital environment, Task View offers a bird's-eye view of your activities, making it easier to focus on the task at hand without the distraction of unrelated applications.

Using Cortana for Voice Commands introduces a level of convenience and accessibility that can be particularly beneficial for seniors. Cortana, Windows 11's built-in digital assistant, enables users to perform a variety of tasks hands-free. Setting up Cortana is a simple process that begins in the settings menu. Navigate to `Settings > Time & Language > Speech`, and ensure the online speech recognition setting is turned on. This feature allows Cortana to understand and process your voice commands more accurately.

Practical uses of Cortana include setting reminders, sending emails, or getting answers to questions without needing to type. To activate Cortana, click on the Cortana icon on the taskbar and then click on the microphone icon in the Cortana window. You can say commands like, "Remind me to call John at 3 PM" or "What's the weather like today?" Cortana's ability to interpret natural language means you don't have to remember specific commands; just speak as if you were talking to another person.

For **Keyboard Shortcuts**, mastering a few key combinations can greatly enhance your efficiency on Windows 11. Beyond the basics of `Ctrl + C` for copy and `Ctrl + V` for paste, there are shortcuts designed to streamline navigation and multitasking. For instance, `Alt + Tab` allows you to switch quickly between open applications, while `Win + L` locks your computer, securing your data when stepping away.

Advanced File Management Techniques involve utilizing File Explorer's more sophisticated features. For example, using the search function in File Explorer can save time. You can refine your searches by using filters such as `date:` or `type:` followed by your search term. This can be particularly useful when looking for specific documents or photos among a large collection. Additionally, right-clicking on files and selecting `Properties` reveals detailed information such as the file size, creation date, and last modified date, which can be helpful for organizing and managing your files.

By integrating these advanced features and customizations into your daily use, Windows 11 becomes not just an operating system, but a powerful tool tailored to your personal and professional needs. These capabilities, when utilized effectively, can simplify complex tasks, enhance productivity, and make the computing experience more enjoyable and suited to your lifestyle.

Virtual Desktops and Task View

To effectively utilize **Virtual Desktops** in Windows 11, one must first understand its core functionality: it allows users to create multiple desktop environments, each tailored for different tasks or projects. This feature is a boon for users seeking to organize their digital workspace without the need to invest in multiple monitors. To create a new virtual desktop, simply press Win + Ctrl + D. This shortcut instantly generates a new, clean desktop, allowing you to segment your work into more manageable chunks. For instance, one desktop could be dedicated to personal use, another for work-related applications, and a third for leisure activities such as browsing or media consumption.

Switching between these desktops is just as straightforward. By pressing Win + Ctrl + Left Arrow or Win + Ctrl + Right Arrow, you can seamlessly navigate between your created desktops. This functionality ensures that transitioning from one task to another is both smooth and efficient, minimizing distractions and enhancing productivity.

Task View is another integral feature that complements Virtual Desktops. Accessed by pressing Win + Tab, Task View provides an overview of all open windows and desktops. It's a visual representation that not only shows what's currently active but also allows for the easy management of virtual desktops. From here, you can add new desktops, close existing ones, or move applications from one desktop to another. This level of control and visualization is particularly useful for seniors, as it simplifies the management of multiple tasks and applications.

For those who frequently use certain applications across all desktops, Windows 11 offers the option to pin apps. Right-clicking on an application's window in Task View and selecting "Show this window on all desktops" ensures that the application is accessible no matter which desktop you're working on. This feature is especially handy for email clients, web browsers, or any tool that you consistently rely upon throughout your computing sessions.

Using Cortana for Voice Commands

Cortana, Windows 11's built-in digital assistant, offers a hands-free way to interact with your computer, making it especially useful for seniors who might prefer speaking over typing or navigating through menus. To start using Cortana for voice commands, you first need to ensure that Cortana is set up and activated on your system. Navigate to the **Settings** menu by pressing Win + I, then select **Cortana** to adjust your preferences, such as speech, inking, and typing personalization, which allows Cortana to better understand your voice commands. It's crucial to have a microphone connected to your computer; most laptops have built-in microphones, but if you're using a desktop, you may need to connect an external one.

Once Cortana is activated, you can invoke it by saying "Hey Cortana," followed by your command. This feature can be enabled in Cortana's settings under the **Talk to Cortana** tab, where you can toggle the **Let Cortana respond to "Hey Cortana"** option. For those concerned about privacy, it's worth noting that you can review and delete your voice activity data in the **Privacy Dashboard** to maintain control over your information.

Cortana can perform a wide range of tasks, from setting reminders and alarms to answering questions about the weather, news, or general knowledge. For example, you can say "Hey Cortana, remind me to call John at 3 PM tomorrow," and Cortana will set a reminder for you. If you're looking for a file on your computer, you can ask, "Hey Cortana, find my document about Windows 11," and Cortana will search your files for a match. This eliminates the need to manually sift through folders, saving time and making your computer use more efficient.

For those who enjoy listening to music or staying updated with the latest news, Cortana can play music and read news headlines with simple voice commands like "Hey Cortana, play my music playlist" or "Hey Cortana, what's the news today?" This integration of Cortana with your digital life makes accessing information and entertainment seamless and straightforward.

Moreover, Cortana can assist with navigating Windows 11 itself. Commands such as "Hey Cortana, open Settings" or "Hey Cortana, increase the volume" allow you to control your computer's settings without lifting a finger. This level of voice control is particularly beneficial for users with mobility challenges or those who prefer a more intuitive interaction with their devices.

Incorporating Cortana into your daily routine can significantly enhance your computing experience, making it more accessible and enjoyable. As you become more familiar with the range of commands Cortana understands, you'll find it an indispensable tool for managing your digital life. Remember, the more you use Cortana, the better it gets at understanding your voice and preferences, thanks to its machine learning capabilities. So, don't hesitate to explore and utilize Cortana to its full potential, as it's designed to make your interaction with Windows 11 as smooth and efficient as possible.

Setting Up Cortana

To initiate the setup of Cortana on your Windows 11 device, the first step involves ensuring that your microphone is properly configured. This is pivotal as Cortana relies on voice commands. Access the **Sound settings** by right-clicking the sound icon on the taskbar and selecting **Sound settings**. Here, verify that your microphone is listed and set as the default device. If you encounter any issues, running the **Troubleshoot** option can help resolve common microphone problems.

With your microphone ready, proceed to activate Cortana by opening the **Settings** app (Win + I), navigating to the **Cortana** section. Here, you'll find various options to customize how Cortana interacts with you. It's advisable to turn on the **Keyboard shortcut** option, which allows you to summon Cortana by pressing Win + C. For hands-free convenience, enabling the **Voice activation** toggle is essential. This setting permits Cortana to listen for the "Hey Cortana" wake phrase. Adjust the **Voice activation privacy settings** to manage how Cortana handles voice data, ensuring a balance between personalization and privacy.

Cortana's capabilities extend beyond mere voice commands; it integrates deeply with your calendar, email, and contacts, provided you grant the necessary permissions. This integration enables Cortana to offer personalized assistance, such as reminding you about upcoming appointments or sending emails on your behalf. To fine-tune these features, delve into the **Permissions** section within Cortana's settings. Select which information Cortana can access to enhance its utility while respecting your privacy preferences.

For a more tailored experience, explore the **Talk to Cortana** feature, where you can customize how Cortana responds to your voice. This includes training Cortana to recognize your voice pattern, significantly improving accuracy in voice recognition. This training process involves reading aloud sentences displayed on the screen, which Cortana uses to learn the nuances of your voice.

Cortana also offers a **Personalization** tab, where you can input critical details about yourself, such as your favorite places (home, work, etc.), which Cortana uses to provide contextually relevant information, like traffic updates for your commute. Additionally, linking your Microsoft account with Cortana enables a seamless experience across devices, allowing Cortana to access your preferences and data securely from the cloud.

Remember, the effectiveness of Cortana hinges on the clarity of your commands. Practice articulating commands distinctly and experiment with different phrases to discover how Cortana best responds. For instance, tasks like setting reminders ("Hey Cortana, remind me to water the plants tomorrow at 9 AM") or querying information ("Hey Cortana, what's the weather like today?") can be accomplished with simple, direct commands.

Finally, it's worth exploring the **Cortana Notebook**, a feature that stores your interests, favorite places, and other personal information. This digital notebook is where Cortana keeps track of your preferences to provide personalized assistance. Regularly updating the Notebook ensures Cortana remains an invaluable assistant that understands your needs and preferences.

By following these steps to set up and personalize Cortana, you harness a powerful tool designed to make your interaction with Windows 11 not only more productive but also more enjoyable. The key to maximizing Cortana's potential lies in continuous use and exploration of its features, allowing it to become more attuned to your preferences and lifestyle.

Practical Uses of Cortana

Cortana's utility extends far beyond basic commands, evolving into a comprehensive assistant that can manage your calendar, send emails, and even control smart home devices. By integrating Cortana with your Microsoft account, you unlock a personalized experience that adapts to your habits and preferences, making everyday tasks simpler and more intuitive. For seniors looking to streamline their digital interactions, Cortana offers a bridge to a more accessible and manageable computing environment.

One of the most practical uses of Cortana is in managing your daily schedule. By simply saying, "Hey Cortana, add a doctor's appointment to my calendar for next Thursday at 10 AM," you can avoid the cumbersome process of manually entering appointments. Cortana's ability to interact with your calendar and provide reminders ensures that you never miss an important date or event. This feature is particularly beneficial for those who maintain a busy schedule or may have difficulty remembering numerous appointments.

Email management is another area where Cortana can significantly enhance productivity. Commands like, "Hey Cortana, send an email to Emily saying, 'Looking forward to our lunch tomorrow!'" allow for quick and hands-free communication. This functionality is especially useful for seniors who may find typing cumbersome or prefer the natural flow of voice communication. Cortana's integration with email services through your Microsoft account means that staying in touch with friends, family, and colleagues is as simple as speaking a command.

For individuals interested in staying informed or entertained, Cortana can curate news, play your favorite music, or even read audiobooks. Saying, "Hey Cortana, play the latest episode of my favorite podcast," turns your computer into a multimedia center, accessible entirely through voice commands. This hands-free access to entertainment and information is not only convenient but also enables seniors to easily engage with digital content without the barrier of complex interfaces or navigation.

Smart home control is another frontier where Cortana excels. By setting up Cortana to work with compatible smart home devices, you can control lighting, adjust thermostats, or check security cameras with simple voice commands. For example, "Hey Cortana, turn on the living room lights," can illuminate your space without the need to physically interact with a switch. This level of control is particularly advantageous for those with mobility issues or anyone looking to create a more responsive living environment.

Moreover, Cortana can serve as a learning tool, answering questions and providing explanations on a wide range of topics. Asking, "Hey Cortana, how do I change the background on my computer?" or "Hey Cortana, what's the capital of France?" offers immediate access to information and step-by-step guidance. This feature not only fosters a sense of independence but also encourages curiosity and continuous learning.

To make the most out of Cortana, it's important to regularly review and adjust its settings in the Cortana Notebook. Personalizing Cortana's responses and the information it has access to ensures that the assistant becomes more attuned to your preferences over time. Additionally, taking advantage of the feedback mechanism to rate Cortana's responses helps improve its accuracy and relevance, making your interactions more efficient and enjoyable.

Cortana's versatility and adaptability make it an invaluable tool for seniors seeking to navigate the digital world with ease. By leveraging Cortana's voice command capabilities, users can enjoy a more accessible, personalized, and engaging computing experience. Whether it's managing your schedule, staying connected, or controlling your smart home, Cortana simplifies technology, making it more approachable and useful for everyday life.

Tips and Tricks for Power Users

Keyboard Shortcuts

Mastering **keyboard shortcuts** in Windows 11 not only boosts productivity but also provides a more streamlined interaction with your computer, particularly beneficial for those who may find traditional navigation methods cumbersome or less efficient. The beauty of keyboard shortcuts lies in their ability to execute commands swiftly without the need to navigate through menus or icons.

For instance, the act of copying and pasting text or files, a fundamental operation for most users, is effortlessly accomplished by pressing `Ctrl + C` to copy and `Ctrl + V` to paste. This method is universally applicable across most applications, making it a vital skill to cultivate. Similarly, if you need to quickly undo an action, `Ctrl + Z` is your go-to shortcut, offering an immediate remedy to most inadvertent changes.

Navigating through files and folders can be significantly expedited using shortcuts as well. Pressing `Win + E` opens the File Explorer, a gateway to your documents, pictures, and other stored data. Once inside the File Explorer, `Ctrl + N` opens a new window, enabling you to view and manage multiple folders simultaneously without losing your place.

For those who frequently engage with digital content, the shortcut `Ctrl + P` opens the print dialog in most applications, allowing for a swift transition from screen to paper. Additionally, capturing a screenshot of your current screen can be done by pressing `Win + PrtScn`, automatically saving the image to your Pictures folder for easy access and sharing.

Multitasking is an integral part of managing a digital lifestyle, and Windows 11 facilitates this through the use of **Virtual Desktops**. Managing these environments becomes intuitive with shortcuts like `Win + Ctrl + D` to create a new desktop and `Win + Ctrl + F4` to close the current desktop. Switching between open applications is also streamlined with `Alt + Tab`, presenting all open applications and allowing you to select the desired one with ease.

For those seeking to access settings or features quickly, `Win + I` opens the Settings menu, a central hub for customizing your Windows 11 experience. When privacy is a concern, or you need to step away momentarily, `Win + L` locks your computer, requiring your password or biometric verification to regain access.

Enhancing accessibility, Windows 11 includes several shortcuts designed to improve the computing experience for users with different needs. `Win + U` opens the Ease of Access Center, providing quick adjustments to make your computer more comfortable to use. For individuals with visual impairments, `Win + Plus` and `Win + Minus` activate the Magnifier, allowing you to zoom in and out on parts of your screen for better visibility.

Incorporating these keyboard shortcuts into your daily use of Windows 11 will not only make your computer more accessible but also transform your interaction into a more efficient and enjoyable experience. Each shortcut, from managing files with `Win + E` to locking your screen with `Win + L`, is designed to minimize effort and maximize productivity. As you become more familiar with these combinations, you'll discover a smoother, more responsive computing environment that caters to your needs and preferences, enhancing not just your efficiency but also your overall digital experience.

Chapter 7: Connecting with Others

In the realm of **Windows 11**, connecting with others has never been more straightforward and enriching, especially with the integration of **Skype** and **Microsoft Teams**. These platforms are designed to bring people closer, whether for personal conversations or professional collaborations. **Skype**, a pioneer in video calling, offers a user-friendly interface that seniors can navigate with ease. To start using Skype, download the app from the Microsoft Store and create an account using a Microsoft email. The process is intuitive: once installed, open Skype and follow the on-screen instructions to set up your profile. Making a video call is as simple as finding the contact you wish to call and clicking the video camera icon.

Microsoft Teams, on the other hand, is more than a video calling application; it's a comprehensive collaboration tool. Initially geared towards businesses, Teams has found a broader audience, offering features like chat, meetings, calls, and collaboration on documents in real time. To get started, download Microsoft Teams from the Microsoft Store, sign in with your Microsoft account, and you're ready to connect. You can join existing teams or create your own and invite friends or family. The interface allows you to easily schedule meetings, share files, and even use virtual backgrounds during video calls.

For those looking to enhance their video call experience, here are some tips:

- **Ensure a stable internet connection** to maintain video quality. Wired connections or strong Wi-Fi signals are preferable.

- **Good lighting** is key. Position yourself so that light sources are in front of you, not behind, to avoid being backlit.

- **Test your audio and video** before the call. Both Skype and Teams have settings to check your microphone and camera.

- **Use headphones** with a microphone for clearer audio, minimizing echo and background noise.

- **Familiarize yourself with the mute and video off buttons** to avoid unintentional disruptions during group calls.

Staying Safe on Social Media: As seniors venture into online communities, safety becomes paramount. Social media platforms are wonderful for staying connected, but it's important to understand privacy settings and recognize common online scams. Always think twice before sharing personal information, and adjust your privacy settings to control who sees your posts. Be wary of messages from strangers, especially those asking for personal or financial information.

Joining and Participating in Online Communities: The internet hosts a plethora of communities for virtually every interest. Whether it's gardening, photography, or technology, there's a community waiting for you. Websites like Reddit and Facebook offer groups where seniors can share their interests, ask questions, and connect with like-minded individuals. When joining these communities, take the time to read the rules and guidelines, and don't hesitate to introduce yourself. Sharing your knowledge and experiences can be incredibly rewarding, and you'll likely learn something new in return.

By embracing these digital tools and platforms, seniors can significantly enhance their social interactions and stay engaged with family, friends, and communities worldwide. Whether it's a video call to catch up with grandchildren or participating in a forum about a favorite hobby, Windows 11 makes these connections seamless and enjoyable.

Video Calls and Meetings

Maximizing the efficiency of **video calls and meetings** on Windows 11 requires a blend of technical setup and best practices. **Optimizing camera and microphone settings** is crucial for clear communication. Access these settings through the **Sound** and **Camera** options in the **Windows Settings** menu. Here, you can adjust the input levels of your microphone and ensure your camera is correctly configured. For those using external devices, it's important to select the correct input and output sources within these settings.

Creating an environment conducive to video calls involves more than just hardware; it also encompasses the physical setup. Positioning the camera at eye level can help simulate a face-to-face conversation, making the interaction more engaging. Additionally, minimizing background noise and ensuring adequate lighting can significantly improve the call quality. For lighting, natural light is preferable, but if that's not possible, a well-placed lamp can illuminate your face evenly.

Leveraging the features of Skype and Microsoft Teams can also enhance your video calling experience. Both platforms offer the ability to **blur or change your**

background, which can be useful if your environment is cluttered or distracting. This option can be found in the video settings before or during a call. Furthermore, familiarizing yourself with the chat and file-sharing features can make sharing information during meetings more seamless. For instance, you can share documents or presentations by clicking the **share icon** during a call.

Scheduling meetings in advance can help manage your time and ensure participants are available. Both Skype and Teams allow you to schedule calls or meetings directly from the app. When scheduling, you have the option to set a reminder, which can be invaluable for staying organized. Additionally, exploring the **meeting recording feature** can be beneficial for those who wish to review the call later or share it with someone who couldn't attend in real time.

Practicing digital etiquette during video calls is also vital. This includes muting your microphone when not speaking to minimize background noise and using the **raise hand feature** in Microsoft Teams to signal when you wish to speak. Such practices can prevent disruptions and ensure the meeting runs smoothly.

For seniors looking to stay connected with family, friends, or colleagues, mastering these aspects of video calls and meetings can make a world of difference. By taking the time to understand and utilize the tools available in Windows 11, users can enjoy rich, fulfilling interactions that bridge the gap between traditional communication and the digital age.

Using Skype and Teams

Delving deeper into the functionalities of Skype and Microsoft Teams, it becomes apparent how these platforms can serve as a lifeline for seniors seeking to maintain connections in the digital age. The integration of these applications within Windows 11 not only simplifies communication but also enriches the user experience with a plethora of features designed to cater to both personal and professional needs.

For instance, organizing a family reunion or a virtual get-together with old friends becomes a breeze with Skype. The platform allows for the creation of group chats where you can easily send out invitations to your contacts. Once everyone is added, initiating a group video call is just a click away. The beauty of Skype lies in its simplicity and its ability to bring people together, irrespective of their geographical locations.

On the other hand, Microsoft Teams offers a more structured environment, ideal for organizing virtual meetings, seminars, or even casual catch-ups. The ability to create different channels within a team allows for the segregation of discussions, making it easier to navigate through topics and keep track of conversations. For those looking to share their knowledge or perhaps host a webinar, Teams provides the tools to do so effectively. You can share your screen to present documents or slides, making it an invaluable tool for educators and professionals alike.

Moreover, both platforms support file sharing, which adds another layer of interaction. Whether it's sharing family photos on Skype or distributing meeting agendas on Teams, the process is straightforward. Simply click on the attachment icon and select the file you wish to share. This feature is particularly useful for collaborative projects, where multiple revisions of documents may need to be exchanged and reviewed.

Another noteworthy feature is the ability to record calls on both Skype and Microsoft Teams. This function is invaluable for those who may want to revisit a family event or for professionals who need to review details of a meeting. To record a call, one simply needs to click on the More options button and select Start recording. The recording is then available for download and can be saved for future reference.

Accessibility features on both platforms also deserve mention, as they play a crucial role in ensuring that everyone, regardless of their abilities, can participate fully. Features such as live captions during video calls make it easier for individuals who are hard of hearing to follow along. Additionally, the high contrast and large text options available in Windows 11 further enhance the usability of Skype and Teams for those with visual impairments.

In leveraging the capabilities of Skype and Microsoft Teams, seniors can effortlessly stay in touch with family, reconnect with old friends, and engage in social activities that were once limited by physical distance. These platforms not only break down geographical barriers but also offer a sense of belonging and community in an increasingly digital world. By taking advantage of these tools, seniors can navigate the complexities of modern communication with confidence, ensuring that they remain an active and integral part of their social circles.

Tips for Better Video Calls

Enhancing the quality of video calls extends beyond the technical adjustments of camera and microphone settings. The **visual composition** of your video frame plays a significant role in creating a more professional and engaging presence. Pay attention to the **rule of thirds**; imagine your screen divided into nine equal segments by two vertical and two horizontal lines. Try to position yourself such that your eyes are approximately on the top horizontal line. This technique not only improves the composition but also makes the interaction feel more natural to the viewer.

Background selection is equally critical. A cluttered or distracting background can divert attention away from the conversation. Utilize the **blur background** feature available in Skype and Microsoft Teams to keep the focus on you. Alternatively, selecting a **virtual background** that is professional and minimalistic can also enhance viewer focus. Ensure the chosen background is appropriate for the context of your call, whether it's a casual chat with friends or a formal business meeting.

Lighting deserves special attention. The goal is to illuminate your face evenly without harsh shadows. Position a light source in front of you, such as a window or a lamp, to achieve this effect. Avoid overhead lighting that can create deep shadows under your eyes. If necessary, consider investing in an affordable **ring light** to achieve consistent lighting regardless of the time of day or room you are in.

The **angle of your camera** is another aspect that can drastically affect the quality of your video calls. A camera placed too low can be unflattering and may give the impression of looking down on others. Adjust your camera or device so that it's at or slightly above eye level, mimicking direct eye contact. This setup helps in fostering a more personal and direct connection with your audience.

Sound quality can make or break a video call. External microphones can significantly improve audio clarity over built-in microphones. When selecting an external microphone, consider a **USB microphone** for ease of use and compatibility with most devices. For environments with unavoidable background noise, a **headset with a noise-cancelling microphone** can help isolate your voice from the surrounding distractions.

Practice active listening during your calls. This not only involves paying attention but also showing that you are engaged. Nodding, maintaining eye contact through the camera, and verbal affirmations signal to the speaker that you are fully present. These cues are crucial in a medium where traditional body language cues are minimized.

Familiarize yourself with the software's features before the call. Knowing how to quickly mute your microphone, turn off your camera, or share your screen can keep the call flowing smoothly. Both Skype and Microsoft Teams offer a range of functionalities designed to enhance collaboration, from **screen sharing** to **real-time document collaboration**. Taking the time to understand these features can greatly improve the efficiency and productivity of your video calls.

Preparation is key to a successful video call. Before the call, close unnecessary applications on your computer to ensure it runs smoothly. Check your internet connection and consider restarting your router if you've been experiencing connectivity issues. Have all relevant documents or websites open and ready to share to avoid awkward pauses during the call.

By integrating these practices into your video calling routine, you can significantly enhance the quality and effectiveness of your communications. Whether connecting with loved ones, attending a virtual meeting, or hosting a webinar, these tips will help you present yourself in the best possible light, making every video call a more productive and enjoyable experience.

Social Media and Online Communities

Navigating the landscape of **social media and online communities** can be a rewarding experience, offering seniors a gateway to connect with others who share their interests and passions. Platforms like **Facebook**, **Instagram**, and **Twitter** provide spaces where one can follow news, engage in discussions, and even participate in group activities or events. To begin, creating an account on these platforms is a straightforward process. For Facebook and Instagram, one can sign up using an email address or a mobile number. Twitter, while similar, asks for a bit more information during the signup process to tailor content to your interests.

Once your account is set up, personalizing your profile is the next step. This involves uploading a profile picture, which could be a recent photo of yourself or something that represents your interests. Adding a brief bio or description about yourself helps others with similar interests find and connect with you. It's also a good practice to follow or join groups that align with your hobbies or passions. For instance, if you're an avid gardener, joining a gardening group on Facebook can provide access to valuable tips, exchange of ideas, and even local gardening events.

Privacy settings are crucial in managing who can see your posts, personal information, and even who can send you friend requests or messages. Each platform has its own set of privacy tools and options, usually found in the settings menu. It's advisable to review these settings regularly to ensure your online experience remains secure and comfortable. For example, you might choose to make your posts visible only to friends on Facebook or opt for a private account on Instagram, where only approved followers can see your content.

Engaging with content on these platforms can vary from liking and commenting on posts to sharing interesting articles, photos, or videos with your network. **Sharing your own content** is also a great way to express yourself and keep friends and family updated on your life. However, it's important to be mindful of the information you share online. Avoid posting sensitive personal information, such as your home address or financial details, to protect against identity theft and scams.

Online communities, such as forums on Reddit or specialized groups on Facebook, offer a more focused environment for discussion and information exchange. These communities often have moderators and set rules to ensure conversations remain respectful and relevant to the topic. Participating in these communities can be incredibly fulfilling, as it allows for deeper engagement with subjects you're passionate about. When joining a new community, take a moment to read through the rules and guidelines, and observe the discussions before jumping in. This helps in understanding the community's culture and etiquette.

For those interested in **learning and sharing knowledge**, platforms like **Quora** or **Stack Exchange** can be invaluable. You can ask questions on a wide range of topics or contribute answers based on your own expertise and experiences. These platforms operate on a system of upvotes and reputation, which helps in highlighting quality responses and contributors.

Staying Safe on Social Media

In the realm of social media, safeguarding one's privacy and security becomes paramount, especially for seniors who are navigating these platforms. The first step in maintaining safety is to meticulously manage privacy settings on each social media account. Platforms like Facebook, Twitter, and Instagram offer comprehensive privacy controls that allow users to determine who can view their posts, photos, and profile information. It's advisable to review these settings regularly, as social media companies often update their policies and settings interfaces.

Another critical aspect is the creation and management of strong passwords. A robust password should be a complex combination of letters, numbers, and symbols, significantly reducing the likelihood of unauthorized access. Tools such as password managers can assist in generating and storing these passwords securely. Additionally, enabling two-factor authentication (2FA) adds an extra layer of security, requiring not only a password and username but also something that only the user has on them, i.e., a piece of information only they should know or have immediately to hand - like a physical token or a text message verification code sent to their mobile phone.

Being cautious about the information shared on social media is equally important. Personal details such as home addresses, phone numbers, or vacation plans should not be shared publicly, as they can be used by malicious actors to harm the user or their property. It's also wise to be skeptical of friend requests from unknown individuals and to avoid clicking on suspicious links, which could lead to phishing sites or malware.

Engaging with social media platforms doesn't have to be a daunting task. By adhering to these safety protocols, seniors can enjoy the benefits of staying connected with family and friends, sharing experiences, and meeting new people with shared interests, all while minimizing the risks associated with online activities. It's about creating a balance between openness and caution, ensuring a positive and secure online social experience.

Joining Online Communities

Upon deciding to join an online community, the initial step involves selecting a platform that aligns with your interests or needs. Whether it's a forum dedicated to gardening enthusiasts, a Facebook group for vintage car collectors, or a subreddit for discussing the latest in technology, the digital world is teeming with niches catering to virtually every interest under the sun. After identifying a suitable community, the process of joining typically requires creating an account. This might involve providing an email address, setting up a username, and choosing a password. Remember, the use of a **strong password** and enabling **two-factor authentication** (2FA) when available is crucial for protecting your online identity.

Once your account is set up, take a moment to familiarize yourself with the community's guidelines or rules. Most online communities have specific regulations regarding posts, comments, and interactions to ensure a respectful and positive environment. Violating these guidelines can result in warnings or even being banned from the community, so it's important to understand what is expected of you as a member.

Engagement within the community can take many forms. You might start by **lurking,** which means reading posts and comments without actively contributing. Lurking allows you to get a feel for the community's culture, the types of discussions that take place, and how members interact with one another. When you feel ready to contribute, begin by commenting on existing threads. This can be a great way to introduce yourself and start engaging with other members. Your comments should add value to the conversation, whether through insight, support, humor, or asking thoughtful questions.

Creating your own posts is another way to participate. Whether you're seeking advice, sharing an experience, or starting a discussion on a topic you're passionate about, original posts are a valuable contribution to the community. Ensure your posts are clear, concise, and formatted in a way that's easy to read; for instance, using **bullet points** or **paragraph breaks** to organize your thoughts can greatly enhance readability.

Active participation also involves voting on content, if the platform offers such a feature. Upvoting posts and comments that you find helpful or enjoyable supports the community by recognizing valuable contributions. Some platforms also allow downvoting for content that doesn't contribute to the discussion or violates community guidelines.

As you become more involved, you may encounter opportunities to take on more significant roles within the community, such as becoming a moderator or organizing virtual events. These roles can be rewarding ways to contribute to the community's health and growth, but they also require a greater commitment and understanding of the community's dynamics.

Remember, the key to a fulfilling experience in online communities lies in mutual respect and contribution. By following these guidelines and actively participating, you can forge meaningful connections, expand your knowledge, and enjoy the rich tapestry of discussions and interactions that online communities offer.

Chapter 8: Entertainment and Hobbies

Windows 11 offers a plethora of **entertainment and hobby** options that cater to a wide range of interests, from digital art creation to gaming and even to exploring new realms of knowledge through reading. For seniors looking to dive into their creative side, **Paint 3D** and **Photos** apps provide intuitive platforms for unleashing artistic talents. Paint 3D, an evolution of the classic Paint application, introduces users to 3D modeling in a user-friendly environment. It allows for the creation of three-dimensional objects from scratch or modifying existing 3D models with tools that are easy to understand and use. The Photos app, on the other hand, is not just for viewing images. It offers powerful editing tools for enhancing pictures, creating albums, and even adding effects to videos, making it a versatile tool for personal media management.

For those interested in writing or blogging, Windows 11 has built-in features that support these activities. The **Microsoft Store** provides access to various applications designed for writers, including distraction-free text editors, grammar checkers, and apps that help organize thoughts and research. These tools are designed to make the writing process as smooth and efficient as possible, catering to both novice writers and seasoned authors.

Gaming on Windows 11 is another area where seniors can find enjoyment and challenge. The Microsoft Store is home to a wide array of games, ranging from casual puzzles to more complex strategy and adventure games. Gaming is not only a fun pastime but also a great way to keep the mind engaged and sharp. Windows 11 is designed to support gaming with features like **Game Mode**, which optimizes system resources for a smoother gaming experience, and **Xbox integration**, which offers access to a vast library of games through Xbox Game Pass.

Exploring these entertainment options on Windows 11 is made easier with the operating system's emphasis on accessibility and ease of use. Features such as **text-to-speech**, **magnifier**, and **high contrast themes** ensure that these activities are accessible to seniors with varying levels of vision. Additionally, the **Ease of Access Center** provides quick adjustments to make the computer more comfortable to use, whether that involves adjusting the size of text and icons or simplifying the navigation.

As seniors embark on exploring these entertainment and hobby options, they'll find that Windows 11 not only offers the tools and features to support their interests but also provides a platform that encourages learning and discovery. Whether it's through creating, playing, or learning, Windows 11 stands as a testament to the idea that technology can be both accessible and engaging, regardless of age.

For individuals keen on staying updated with the latest news or diving into the world of literature, Windows 11 offers an enriching experience through its **Reading eBooks and News** feature. The **Microsoft Edge** browser is equipped with a built-in **eBook reader** that supports various formats, allowing users to easily access and read their favorite books directly within the browser. Additionally, the **News** app curates articles from reputable sources, tailored to the user's interests, ensuring they stay informed on current events and topics of personal interest. This integration of reading materials directly into the operating system makes it convenient for seniors to indulge in reading without the need for additional devices or applications.

Moreover, Windows 11 enhances the **streaming music and videos** experience with its compatibility with popular services like **Spotify** and **Netflix** through apps available in the Microsoft Store. These apps are designed with user-friendly interfaces, making it easy for seniors to navigate and enjoy their favorite shows, movies, and music playlists. The **Groove Music** app also offers a platform for organizing and playing music files stored on the computer, providing a seamless listening experience.

The **Photos** app goes beyond just viewing and editing images; it also serves as a digital storytelling tool. Users can create **video projects** combining photos, video clips, and music to share memories and stories with family and friends. This feature is particularly appealing for seniors looking to document life's moments or share experiences with loved ones who may be far away.

In the realm of **social media and online communities**, Windows 11 facilitates easy access and management of social media accounts, enabling seniors to stay connected with their social circles and engage in communities that share their interests. The integration of **social media apps** within the operating system allows for notifications and updates to be readily accessible, ensuring users never miss an important message or post.

Lastly, Windows 11 acknowledges the importance of **health and well-being** by offering apps that focus on fitness, meditation, and mindfulness. The **Microsoft Store** includes apps like **MyFitnessPal** and **Headspace**, which provide resources for maintaining physical health and mental well-being. These apps offer guided exercises, nutrition tracking, and meditation sessions that can be easily incorporated into daily routines, highlighting the operating system's role in supporting a balanced lifestyle.

Through these diverse entertainment and hobby features, Windows 11 proves to be a versatile platform that caters to the varied interests of senior users. It underscores the operating system's commitment to providing accessible, enjoyable, and enriching experiences, empowering seniors to explore their interests, stay informed, and connect with others, all while prioritizing ease of use and accessibility.

Exploring Windows 11 for Creativity

Windows 11 is equipped with a suite of applications and features designed to foster creativity, among which **3D Viewer** and **Snip & Sketch** stand out for their utility and ease of access. **3D Viewer** allows users to view and interact with 3D models, providing a hands-on experience that can be particularly engaging for those interested in digital art or design. This application supports a variety of file formats, enabling users to explore a wide range of 3D creations. To open a model in **3D Viewer**, simply search for the app in the Start menu, then select `File` > `Open` to choose a 3D model from your files.

Snip & Sketch, on the other hand, offers a quick and efficient way to capture and annotate screenshots. This tool is invaluable for creating tutorials, explaining steps in a process, or simply sharing information in a visual format. To use **Snip & Sketch**, press `Windows` + `Shift` + `S` to activate the snipping bar, allowing you to select the area of your screen you wish to capture. Once taken, the screenshot can be annotated using a variety of tools within the app, such as a pen, pencil, highlighter, and more. The annotated image can then be saved, copied, or shared directly from **Snip & Sketch**.

For those with a passion for photography or graphic design, **Adobe Photoshop Elements** available through the Microsoft Store, offers a user-friendly interface combined with powerful editing tools. Photoshop Elements caters to both beginners and experienced users, with guided edits for newcomers and advanced features for more seasoned creators. This software provides a comprehensive toolkit for photo editing, from basic adjustments like cropping and color correction to more complex manipulations such as layering and blending modes.

Music enthusiasts will appreciate the capabilities of **Groove Music** and **Spotify**, both accessible on Windows 11. **Groove Music** serves as a music player for your digital library, allowing you to organize and play your favorite tracks and albums. For a more expansive selection, **Spotify** offers streaming access to a vast library of songs, playlists, and podcasts. Both apps support creating custom playlists, offering a personalized listening experience. To get started, download **Spotify** from the Microsoft Store and log in with your account, or open **Groove Music** and import your music collection by selecting `Settings` > `Music on this PC`.

Lastly, **Windows Ink Workspace** presents a canvas for digital pen users, providing tools such as **Sketchpad**, **Screen Sketch**, and **Sticky Notes**. These tools are perfect for jotting down ideas, sketching out designs, or annotating documents and images. To access **Windows Ink Workspace**, click the pen icon on the taskbar or press `Windows` + `W`. Here, you can choose the tool that best suits your current project or task.

Each of these features and applications in Windows 11 is designed with the user in mind, offering intuitive interfaces and robust functionalities that cater to a wide range of creative pursuits. Whether you're drawing, designing, writing, or making music, Windows 11 provides the tools you need to explore your creativity and bring your ideas to life.

Using Paint 3D and Photos

Paint 3D, a successor to the classic Paint application, revolutionizes the way we think about digital art by introducing an intuitive platform for creating three-dimensional masterpieces. This application is not merely about adding another dimension to your creations; it's about bringing your ideas to life in a way that was previously accessible only to professionals with specialized software. To start with Paint 3D, you simply need to locate it in your Start menu. Upon launching, you're greeted with a clean, user-friendly interface that encourages experimentation. Creating a new project in Paint 3D is as simple as clicking the `New` button. From there, you can use tools like `3D Objects` to add pre-made shapes to your canvas or `3D Doodle` to draw shapes that automatically turn into

3D models. The magic of Paint 3D lies in its simplicity; with straightforward drag-and-drop controls, you can rotate and resize your 3D models with ease, making it a perfect tool for seniors looking to explore their creative side without the steep learning curve of more complex software.

The Photos app, on the other hand, serves as a powerful companion in managing and enhancing your digital photo collection. Beyond its capability to organize your photos, the app offers a robust set of editing tools that can transform your snapshots into polished, gallery-worthy pieces. To edit a photo, simply open it within the Photos app and select the `Edit & Create` option from the top menu. Here, you'll find options to crop, rotate, add filters, and adjust lighting and color. One of the standout features of the Photos app is its `Enhance your photo` button, which automatically adjusts your photo to look its best with a single click. For those interested in more granular control, the `Adjustments` menu offers sliders for brightness, contrast, saturation, and more, enabling you to fine-tune your images with precision.

Both Paint 3D and the Photos app exemplify Windows 11's commitment to accessibility and ease of use, making them ideal for seniors eager to delve into digital creativity. Whether you're sculpting your first 3D model or enhancing a cherished family photo, these applications provide a gateway to artistic expression that is both fulfilling and fun. The key to mastering these tools lies in exploration and practice; with each project, you'll discover new techniques and unlock more of your creative potential. Paint 3D and Photos not only stand as testament to Windows 11's capabilities in facilitating creative endeavors but also empower users to see their world in new and exciting ways, all without leaving the comfort of their home computer.

Writing and Blogging Tools

For seniors embarking on the journey of writing and blogging, Windows 11 provides a suite of tools designed to streamline the creative process, making it more accessible and enjoyable. Among these, the built-in **WordPad** application stands as a testament to simplicity and efficiency. WordPad, while less complex than Microsoft Word, offers ample features for composing blog posts, articles, and short stories. Its user-friendly interface is ideal for those who prefer a straightforward writing experience without the clutter of advanced formatting options. To launch WordPad, simply type WordPad into the search bar adjacent to the Start menu and select the app from the search results. Once opened, you'll find a clean workspace ready to capture your thoughts and stories.

For writers seeking a more robust platform, **Microsoft Word**, available through the Microsoft 365 subscription, offers an extensive array of tools for document creation and editing. Microsoft Word caters to both novice and experienced writers with features such as spell check, grammar suggestions, style guides, and templates. These functionalities not only enhance the writing process but also ensure that the final product is polished and professional. To access Microsoft Word, navigate to the Microsoft Store, where you can subscribe to Microsoft 365 or download the app if you already have a subscription. Upon launching Word, you'll be greeted with an array of templates ranging from blank documents to structured layouts for specific writing projects, providing a solid foundation to start from.

Another invaluable resource for writers is **OneNote**, a digital notebook that excels in organizing research, jotting down ideas, and drafting articles. OneNote's flexible canvas allows you to place text, images, and links anywhere on the page, making it an ideal tool for collecting and organizing research materials or brainstorming ideas for your next blog post. With its ability to create multiple notebooks and sections, OneNote serves as an excellent repository for all your writing projects and inspirations. To begin with OneNote, search for it in the Start menu and open the app. From there, you can create a new notebook dedicated to your writing endeavors, with sections for each project or topic you're exploring.

For those who prefer dictating their thoughts, Windows 11's **Voice Typing** feature offers a hands-free writing experience. Voice Typing leverages advanced speech recognition technology to accurately transcribe spoken words into text, making it a powerful tool for quickly capturing ideas or drafting content without the need for typing. To activate Voice Typing, press Windows + H on your keyboard in any text field within Windows 11, and begin speaking. This feature is particularly useful for drafting blog posts or capturing inspiration as it strikes, without being tethered to the keyboard.

In addition to these native tools, the Microsoft Store hosts a variety of third-party applications designed to enhance the writing and blogging experience. Apps like **Scrivener** and **Ulysses** offer advanced features tailored to writers, including manuscript organization, distraction-free writing environments, and export options for various formats and platforms. These applications cater to the needs of serious writers and bloggers who require more functionality than what's available in basic text editors. To explore these options, open the Microsoft Store from your Start menu and search for writing or blogging tools. Here, you'll find detailed descriptions and user reviews to help you select the app that best fits your writing style and needs.

By leveraging these writing and blogging tools available on Windows 11, seniors can easily transform their thoughts and stories into written form, whether for personal fulfillment or sharing with a wider audience. The operating system's emphasis on accessibility and user-friendly design ensures that individuals of all skill levels can navigate these tools with confidence, turning the daunting task of writing into a manageable and enjoyable activity. With Windows 11, the barriers to expressing oneself through writing are significantly reduced, empowering seniors to share their knowledge, experiences, and creativity with the world.

Gaming on Windows 11

Windows 11 brings a plethora of gaming features designed to enhance the gaming experience for users of all ages, especially seniors who are looking to dive into the world of digital entertainment. With the introduction of **Game Mode**, Windows 11 ensures that your system resources are optimized for gaming, providing a smoother and more enjoyable gameplay experience. This feature can be easily activated by going to Settings > Gaming > Game Mode and toggling it on. This prioritizes your gaming applications, ensuring they receive the maximum amount of system resources available.

Another significant integration is with **Xbox**, which is a boon for gamers. The Xbox app on Windows 11 not only allows you to play games but also to connect with friends and join communities, making gaming a more social experience. Through the Xbox app, you can access Xbox Game Pass, a subscription service that offers a vast library of games to download and play on your PC. Setting up the Xbox app is straightforward: simply search for the Xbox app in the Microsoft Store and follow the installation instructions. Once installed, log in with your Microsoft account, and you're ready to explore the world of gaming on Windows 11.

For those interested in accessibility, Windows 11 has made significant strides in making gaming more accessible to everyone. Features such as **Narrator**, which reads out text on the screen, and **Magnifier**, which can enlarge parts of the screen, are invaluable tools for gamers who may have visual impairments. These tools can be easily accessed through the Ease of Access Center in the control panel.

Moreover, Windows 11 has enhanced the compatibility with various gaming peripherals, ensuring that connecting new controllers or gaming keyboards is as simple as plugging them into your PC. The operating system automatically recognizes the device and installs the necessary drivers, allowing you to jump straight into the action without the hassle of manual setup.

For those looking to customize their gaming experience, Windows 11 offers various settings that can be adjusted to suit your preferences. From adjusting graphic settings to optimizing sound quality, these customizations can be accessed through the Settings menu under System and Sound options, respectively.

Lastly, the Microsoft Store has become a central hub for discovering new games. With a user-friendly interface and a wide selection of titles, finding games that suit your interests has never been easier. Whether you're into puzzle games, adventure, or action, the Microsoft Store has something for everyone. Regular updates and promotions also mean that you can often find great deals on popular titles.

In summary, Windows 11 has significantly enhanced the gaming experience for users, making it more accessible, enjoyable, and social. With features like Game Mode, Xbox integration, and improved accessibility options, seniors can easily dive into the world of gaming and enjoy everything it has to offer.

Discovering Games in Microsoft Store

Once you've set up the Xbox app and familiarized yourself with Game Mode, venturing into the Microsoft Store to discover new games becomes an exciting next step. The Microsoft Store, accessible directly from your Windows 11 taskbar or Start menu, is a treasure trove of digital entertainment, offering a wide array of games that cater to various interests and skill levels. From brain-teasing puzzle games to adrenaline-pumping action adventures, the Store is designed to make game discovery an effortless experience.

Navigating the Microsoft Store is intuitive. Upon opening the Store, you'll find a dedicated Gaming section. This area is curated to showcase featured games, new releases, and collections based on genres or themes, such as strategy games or family-friendly options. Each game's page provides detailed information, including a description, user reviews, and system requirements, ensuring you make informed decisions about which games might suit your interests and computer capabilities.

For those keen on trying out games without immediate commitment, the Microsoft Store offers free-to-play titles and demos. Free-to-play games are full versions that are available at no cost, often supported by in-game purchases, while demos provide a snippet of the game for you to try before deciding to purchase the full version. To find these, you can filter your search results by selecting Free under the Price filter, or look for tags that say Demo available.

When you find a game that piques your interest, downloading it is straightforward. Click on the game to visit its page, then select Get or Buy, depending on whether the game is free or paid. If it's your first purchase, you may be prompted to enter payment information, which will be securely stored for future transactions. After the purchase, the game will begin downloading, and once completed, it's ready to play directly from your Start menu or through the Xbox app.

Keeping your games updated is also hassle-free. The Microsoft Store automatically checks for updates and, depending on your settings, may download them in the background or notify you when an update is available. This ensures that your games are always up to date with the latest features and security enhancements.

For seniors looking to expand their gaming library, the Microsoft Store also periodically offers deals and discounts on various titles. Checking the Deals section regularly can help you find your next favorite game at a fraction of the cost. Additionally, subscribing to the Xbox Game Pass through the Microsoft Store provides access to a vast library of games for a monthly fee, allowing you to explore a wide range of titles without having to purchase each individually.

The Microsoft Store's integration with Windows 11 and its user-friendly interface make it an ideal platform for seniors to discover and enjoy new games. With the convenience of digital downloads, automatic updates, and a broad selection of titles, the Store is a gateway to countless hours of entertainment tailored to your preferences and skill level. Whether you're a seasoned gamer or new to the digital gaming world, the Microsoft Store on Windows 11 offers a seamless and enjoyable gaming discovery experience.

Enjoying Games Safely and Responsibly

Engaging in the digital gaming world offers a plethora of benefits, including cognitive stimulation, social interaction, and simply the joy of entertainment. However, it's paramount to approach gaming with a mindset geared towards safety and responsibility, especially for seniors who might be navigating these waters for the first time. Here are some essential tips to ensure a positive and secure gaming experience on Windows 11.

Firstly, it's crucial to be aware of the time spent gaming. While it's easy to become engrossed in a game, setting limits can help maintain a healthy balance between digital and real-world activities. Utilize features like the `Alarms & Clock` app on Windows 11 to set reminders to take breaks, stretch, or engage in other activities. This not only helps in avoiding prolonged periods of inactivity but also in preventing digital eye strain, a common issue that can arise from extended screen time.

Another aspect to consider is the social element of online gaming. Many games offer the ability to interact with other players from around the globe, which can be a fantastic way to meet new people and foster friendships. However, it's essential to safeguard personal information. Never share sensitive details like your full name, address, or financial information with fellow gamers. Adjust privacy settings within games and on gaming platforms to control who can see your profile or send you messages. For example, the Xbox app allows you to customize these settings under the `Privacy & online safety` section, ensuring you're only sharing what you're comfortable with.

In addition to privacy concerns, online environments can sometimes expose players to inappropriate content or behavior. Utilize built-in reporting features to alert moderators about any offensive or harmful interactions. Familiarize yourself with each game's community guidelines to understand what is considered acceptable behavior and how to report violations. This proactive approach contributes to a safer gaming environment for everyone.

Financial safety is another critical area. Free-to-play games and in-game purchases can sometimes lead to unexpected expenses. Always review the details of any transaction within a game or on the Microsoft Store. Set up purchase confirmations and spend limits if available. For those who enjoy exploring new games, consider a subscription service like Xbox Game Pass, which offers access to a wide range of games for a flat monthly fee, providing a cost-effective way to enjoy gaming without the worry of individual purchases.

Lastly, the aspect of cybersecurity should not be overlooked. Ensure your Windows 11 system is always up to date with the latest security updates to protect against malware and other online threats. Use reputable antivirus software and be wary of clicking on links or downloading content from unknown sources within gaming platforms or emails. Regularly changing passwords and enabling two-factor authentication (2FA) on gaming accounts adds an extra layer of security.

By adhering to these guidelines, seniors can fully enjoy the immersive world of gaming on Windows 11 while minimizing risks. Gaming should be a source of fun and enrichment, not stress or harm. With the right precautions in place, the digital gaming experience can be both enjoyable and secure, allowing seniors to explore new worlds, challenge their minds, and connect with others in a safe and responsible manner.

Chapter 9: Health and Well-Being

In the realm of **health and well-being**, Windows 11 offers a suite of **apps** that cater to a variety of needs, from **fitness tracking** to **mental health support**. Among these, **MyFitnessPal** provides a comprehensive platform for monitoring diet and exercise, allowing users to set and track goals related to weight, nutrition, and physical activity. The app's database includes nutritional information for millions of foods, making it easier to log meals and snacks. Additionally, MyFitnessPal can sync with other fitness devices and apps, offering a centralized view of your health data.

Headspace, on the other hand, focuses on mental well-being through guided meditations, sleep stories, and mindfulness exercises. Its user-friendly interface encourages daily practice, contributing to stress reduction and improved sleep quality. Both MyFitnessPal and Headspace are available for download from the **Microsoft Store**, ensuring easy installation and access.

For those interested in maintaining an active lifestyle, Windows 11 includes built-in features that support **ergonomic health**. Adjusting your computer setup for comfort can significantly reduce the risk of strain and injury. The **Ease of Access Center** offers settings like **text size adjustment** and **screen brightness control**, which can help in creating a more comfortable computing environment, especially for users with visual impairments.

Moreover, incorporating **regular breaks** into your computer use can prevent **digital eye strain** and **muscle fatigue**. Applications like **Microsoft To-Do** can be used to schedule short breaks for stretching or eye exercises, promoting a healthier routine. Additionally, the **Alarms & Clock** app can remind you to take these breaks at regular intervals, ensuring you maintain a balance between productivity and health.

Customizing for eye comfort is another critical aspect, with Windows 11 providing **Night Light** settings that reduce blue light exposure in the evening hours. This feature can be activated by going to `Settings > System > Display > Night Light settings`, helping to improve sleep quality.

Lastly, the **Windows 11** ecosystem encourages exploration of new hobbies and interests that can contribute to overall well-being. Whether it's learning a new skill through educational apps, exploring creative outlets like **Paint 3D**, or engaging in digital communities, Windows 11 facilitates a balanced and enriching digital experience. Engaging with technology in a way that supports physical and mental health is key to enjoying the benefits of the digital age, especially for seniors seeking to enhance their quality of life through informed and mindful use of their devices.

Staying Healthy with Windows 11

Windows 11 also offers a variety of **ergonomic settings** that can be tailored to reduce physical strain and enhance comfort during computer use. For seniors spending significant time at their computers, adjusting these settings can make a substantial difference in maintaining physical health. The **Ease of Access Center** provides options such as **keyboard customization**, allowing for **Sticky Keys** or **Filter Keys** to be enabled, which can be particularly beneficial for those with limited hand mobility or dexterity issues. To access these features, navigate to `Settings > Ease of Access > Keyboard`. Here, you can enable **Sticky Keys** by toggling the switch, allowing you to press one key at a time for keyboard shortcuts, or turn on **Filter Keys** to ignore brief or repeated keystrokes.

Visual aids are another critical aspect of ergonomics within Windows 11. The operating system includes features like **text enlargement** and **screen magnification**, which can help reduce eye strain for users with visual impairments. To adjust text size, go to `Settings > Ease of Access > Display` and use the slider to increase the text size across the system, apps, and other items. For magnification, the **Magnifier tool** can be activated by pressing `Windows + Plus sign (+)`, allowing you to zoom in on parts of your screen for better visibility.

Voice control and **speech recognition** capabilities in Windows 11 further reduce the need for physical interaction with the device, offering a hands-free experience that can prevent strain and fatigue. To set up speech recognition, navigate to `Settings > Ease of Access > Speech`, where you can activate **Windows Speech Recognition**. This feature enables you to control your computer using voice commands, from opening applications to dictating text, providing a restful alternative to typing or navigating with a mouse.

Maintaining a **healthy posture** while using your computer is essential. Windows 11 can assist with this by supporting the use of multiple monitors, allowing you to position screens at eye level and reduce neck strain. To configure multiple displays, right-click on your desktop and select `Display settings`, where you can arrange your monitors to match their physical setup and adjust their orientation and resolution for optimal viewing comfort.

Regular breaks are vital for physical well-being, and Windows 11 can help remind you to take them. Utilizing the **Alarms & Clock** app, you can set up recurring alarms or timers to encourage you to stand, stretch, or take a brief walk, mitigating the risks associated with prolonged sitting. Open the **Alarms & Clock** app from the Start menu, and in the `Timer` tab, you can create custom timers for break reminders throughout your day.

Incorporating these ergonomic practices and utilizing the health-oriented features of Windows 11 can significantly contribute to a healthier computing experience. By customizing settings to meet individual needs, seniors can enjoy the benefits of technology while minimizing physical discomfort and strain, promoting a balanced and health-conscious approach to computer use.

Health and Fitness Apps

Expanding upon the foundation of health and well-being within the Windows 11 ecosystem, a deeper exploration into the **Microsoft Store** reveals a treasure trove of health and fitness apps designed to cater to a broad spectrum of wellness goals. These applications range from **dietary tracking** to **exercise tutorials**, each offering unique features to assist users in maintaining a healthy lifestyle. For instance, apps like **Fitbit** and **Strava** integrate seamlessly with wearable devices, enabling users to monitor their physical activities and track progress over time. This synchronization between devices and applications not only simplifies the tracking process but also provides a comprehensive overview of one's health metrics directly on their Windows 11 device.

Moreover, for individuals focused on nutritional health, applications such as **Yummly** and **Allrecipes** offer an extensive database of recipes that cater to various dietary preferences and restrictions. These apps provide detailed nutritional information for each recipe, making it easier for users to adhere to specific dietary goals. The convenience of having such resources readily available on a Windows 11 device encourages a more engaged and proactive approach to nutritional planning.

In addition to physical health, mental well-being is another critical aspect that is well-addressed by the Windows 11 platform. Apps like **Calm** and **Sanvello** offer guided meditations, breathing exercises, and cognitive behavioral therapy techniques to help users manage stress and anxiety. The accessibility of these mental health tools on a personal computer can significantly enhance the ease with which individuals incorporate mindfulness and relaxation into their daily routines.

For seniors particularly, the integration of health and fitness apps into their Windows 11 devices can be a game-changer in managing and improving their health. The ability to access a variety of health-related resources from the comfort of their home not only provides convenience but also empowers them to take control of their health and well-being. Furthermore, many of these apps offer customizable settings to accommodate different levels of physical ability and health concerns, ensuring that users can find suitable exercises and activities that match their individual needs.

The **Microsoft Health Dashboard**, accessible through Windows 11, further enhances the user experience by aggregating data from various health and fitness apps into a centralized platform. This dashboard provides a holistic view of the user's health, including activity levels, sleep patterns, and dietary habits, allowing for a more informed approach to health management. By reviewing this consolidated data, users can identify areas for improvement and adjust their health strategies accordingly.

To facilitate the discovery and management of these health and fitness apps, Windows 11 includes a **Device Management** feature that simplifies the process of connecting and managing compatible devices, such as fitness trackers and smartwatches. Through the Settings > Devices menu, users can effortlessly pair their devices with their PC, ensuring that all health data is synchronized and up-to-date.

The commitment of Windows 11 to supporting health and well-being is evident in its comprehensive suite of health and fitness apps available through the Microsoft Store. By leveraging these tools, seniors can enjoy a more active, informed, and balanced lifestyle, demonstrating the operating system's potential as a valuable ally in the pursuit of health and happiness. The integration of these applications with Windows 11 not only underscores the versatility of the platform but also highlights its role in facilitating access to health and wellness resources, making it an indispensable tool for users dedicated to maintaining their health.

Ergonomics and Computer Use

Ergonomics in computer use is a critical consideration for maintaining health and well-being, especially for seniors who may spend considerable time in front of a screen. Proper ergonomic practices can significantly reduce the risk of strain injuries and improve overall comfort during computer use. One of the foundational elements of computer ergonomics is the setup of the physical workspace. The monitor should be positioned at eye level or slightly below to prevent neck strain. This can be achieved by adjusting the monitor stand or using books to elevate the monitor to the appropriate height. The top of the screen should be at or just below eye level, allowing the eyes to naturally look slightly downward when viewing the middle of the screen.

The distance of the monitor from the eyes is another vital aspect; it should be about an arm's length away. This distance helps in reducing eye strain, as it is a comfortable range for the eyes to focus on the screen without exerting extra effort. If text size becomes an issue at this distance, adjusting the display settings in Windows 11 to increase text size can provide relief without needing to move closer to the screen.

Keyboard and mouse placement is equally important in an ergonomic setup. The keyboard should be positioned so that when typing, the forearms are parallel to the floor or slightly tilted downwards, and the wrists are not bending up, down, or to the side. A cushioned wrist rest can help maintain this neutral position, though it should be used sparingly to avoid constant pressure on the underside of the wrists, which can lead to other issues. The mouse should be at the same level as the keyboard and close enough to prevent overreaching, which can strain the shoulder and arm.

Chair selection and positioning play a crucial role in maintaining an ergonomic posture. An adjustable chair that supports the natural curve of the spine is ideal. Feet should rest flat on the floor or on a footrest, with thighs parallel to the floor. The chair should allow the user to sit back comfortably with the lower back supported by the chair's lumbar support, promoting a slight recline which is less taxing on the spine than sitting upright or leaning forward.

In addition to physical setup, taking regular breaks is essential for preventing fatigue and strain. The 20-20-20 rule is a helpful guideline: every 20 minutes, take 20 seconds to look at something 20 feet away. This practice helps in reducing eye strain from prolonged screen time. Windows 11 can assist in this practice through the use of the Alarms & Clock app to set reminders for taking breaks.

Adjusting the brightness and contrast settings on the monitor to match the ambient lighting in the room can also reduce eye strain. Windows 11 offers adaptive brightness settings that can automatically adjust the screen based on the lighting conditions, which can be particularly beneficial for users moving between different environments or using the computer at different times of the day.

Incorporating these ergonomic practices into computer use can significantly enhance comfort and reduce the risk of strain or injury. While it may require some adjustments and getting used to new positions, the long-term health benefits are well worth the effort.

Mindfulness and Relaxation

Incorporating **mindfulness and relaxation** techniques into daily life can significantly enhance mental well-being, especially for seniors navigating the complexities of modern technology. Windows 11 offers a variety of tools and apps that can facilitate these practices, turning the computer into a sanctuary of calm and focus. One such feature is the **Focus Assist** setting, which minimizes distractions by silencing notifications, allowing for a more mindful interaction with technology. To activate Focus Assist, go to `Settings > System > Focus Assist` and select your preferred level of quiet. For those interested in meditation, the **Microsoft Store** hosts an array of apps designed to guide users through meditation sessions. Apps like **Mindful Meditation** and **Calm** provide structured meditation paths, ranging from beginner to advanced levels, and can be easily installed by searching their names in the Microsoft Store and clicking `Install`.

Another tool for relaxation is the **Alarms & Clock** app, not only useful for setting reminders to take breaks but also for practicing the Pomodoro Technique—a time management method that alternates focused work sessions with short breaks. This can be set up by opening the Alarms & Clock app, going to the `Timer` tab, and creating a new timer for 25 minutes of work followed by a 5-minute break. Repeating this cycle can help maintain a steady rhythm of work and rest, promoting mental clarity and reducing stress.

For those who find relaxation in creativity, Windows 11 includes **Paint 3D**, an app that offers a playful and intuitive interface for 3D modeling. Engaging in creative activities like 3D modeling can be a form of mindful relaxation, focusing the mind on the task at hand and providing a break from routine. To start with Paint 3D, simply type `Paint 3D` in the Windows search bar and select the app to open it. Inside, you'll find tools to create custom 3D objects, modify pre-existing models, and share your creations with others.

Lastly, customizing the **theme and background** settings in Windows 11 can also contribute to a more relaxing and personalized computing environment. Changing the desktop background to a serene image or setting a calming color scheme can have subtle yet profound effects on daily computer use. To adjust these settings, navigate to `Settings > Personalization` and explore the options under `Background` and `Colors`. Whether it's a photo of a tranquil landscape or a solid, soothing color, these visual cues can help create a more peaceful and focused workspace.

By leveraging these features and apps, seniors can transform their Windows 11 experience into one that supports mindfulness and relaxation, integrating these practices into their interaction with technology. These tools not only enhance the usability of Windows 11 for seniors but also promote a healthier, more balanced approach to computing.

Meditation and Mindfulness Apps

Expanding the repertoire of tools for mindfulness and meditation, Windows 11 users have at their disposal a variety of applications that cater specifically to enhancing mental well-being through guided meditation, breathing exercises, and mindfulness practices. Among these, **Headspace** stands out as a premier choice, offering a wide range of meditation sessions tailored to different needs and durations. Users can find Headspace by searching for it in the Microsoft Store and clicking `Install`. Once installed, the app provides personalized meditation journeys, which can be particularly beneficial for individuals seeking stress reduction, improved sleep, or enhanced concentration.

Another noteworthy application is **Insight Timer**, which boasts a vast library of free meditations led by mindfulness experts from around the globe. Insight Timer caters to users of all experience levels, from beginners to seasoned practitioners, and covers topics such as anxiety relief, mindfulness at work, and focus. To access Insight Timer, users can search for the app in the Microsoft Store and follow the simple installation process. The app also features a timer for silent meditation, allowing users to customize the length of their meditation sessions and choose ambient sounds to accompany their practice.

For those interested in incorporating mindfulness into their daily routine, **MyLife Meditation** (formerly known as Stop, Breathe & Think) is an excellent option. This app encourages users to check in with their emotions and provides recommended meditations based on their current feelings. MyLife Meditation offers guided sessions for mindfulness, sleep, and emotions, making it a versatile tool for personal well-being. Installation is straightforward via the Microsoft Store, and the app includes a variety of free content, with additional resources available through a subscription.

In addition to dedicated meditation and mindfulness apps, Windows 11 supports the integration of wellness activities into the digital environment through its calendar and reminder functionalities. Users can schedule regular meditation sessions using the **Calendar** app, setting up notifications to remind them to take breaks for mindfulness exercises throughout the day. This can be particularly useful for establishing a consistent meditation practice, ensuring that time is set aside for mental health amidst a busy schedule.

Furthermore, the **Your Phone** app on Windows 11 allows users to stay connected with their mobile devices, providing access to health and wellness apps they may already be using on their smartphones. This seamless integration ensures that users can continue their mindfulness practices without interruption, whether they are on their computer or on the go.

By leveraging these meditation and mindfulness apps, along with the built-in features of Windows 11, seniors can enhance their mental well-being and navigate the challenges of modern technology with greater ease and resilience. These tools not only offer a pathway to relaxation and stress relief but also empower users to take an active role in managing their mental health, fostering a sense of control and well-being in the digital age.

Customizing for Eye Comfort and Sleep

Ensuring eye comfort and promoting better sleep patterns are critical aspects of using technology, especially for seniors who might find prolonged screen time to be straining. Windows 11 is equipped with features designed to mitigate these issues, allowing for a more comfortable computing experience. One such feature is the Night Light setting, which reduces the amount of blue light emitted by the screen. Blue light is known for its potential to disrupt sleep patterns by interfering with the body's natural circadian rhythms. By activating Night Light, users can add a warm tone to their screen, making it easier on the eyes and conducive to better sleep. To enable Night Light, navigate to `Settings > System > Display` and toggle the Night Light switch to `On`. Users can also schedule Night Light to turn on automatically at sunset or at a specific time, adapting to individual routines and preferences.

Another consideration for eye comfort is the text size and overall display scaling. Reading small text can be a strain, leading to eye fatigue. Windows 11 allows users to adjust the scale and layout of their display, making text, apps, and other items easier to see without compromising the sharpness or clarity of the image. To adjust these settings, go to `Settings > System > Display` and find the Scale and layout section. Here, you can change the size of text, apps, and other items to a percentage that suits your visual comfort. For those who need even larger text, the option to `Make text bigger` under the Ease of Access settings provides a slider to increase the text size independently of other elements on the screen.

The clarity of text is another factor that can impact eye comfort. ClearType Text Tuner is a tool within Windows 11 designed to make text easier to read on your screen. By adjusting the way fonts are displayed to suit your monitor, ClearType can significantly enhance readability. To access ClearType Text Tuner, type `ClearType` in the Windows search bar and select `Adjust ClearType text`. Follow the on-screen instructions to tune the text on your screen for better clarity.

In addition to these settings, the overall brightness of the screen should be adjusted according to the ambient light in your environment to reduce eye strain. Windows 11 offers adaptive brightness settings for devices with light sensors, automatically adjusting the screen brightness based on the lighting conditions. However, users can manually adjust screen brightness by going to `Settings > System > Display` and moving the Brightness slider to a comfortable level.

For users who spend extended periods at the computer, it's also beneficial to adopt the practice of taking regular breaks to rest the eyes. The Pomodoro Technique, as mentioned earlier, can be facilitated through the Alarms & Clock app, but simply remembering to look away from the screen every 20 minutes, focusing on a distant object for at least 20 seconds, can help in reducing eye strain. This practice, known as the 20-20-20 rule, is highly recommended by eye care professionals.

By customizing Windows 11 settings to suit individual needs for eye comfort and sleep, users can enjoy a more pleasant computing experience. These adjustments, combined with mindful practices around screen time, can significantly contribute to reducing eye strain and promoting better sleep, enhancing overall well-being for seniors as they engage with technology.

🎁 YOUR EXCLUSIVE BONUS GIFT! 🎁

Thank you for purchasing *Windows 11 for Seniors* by Tony Mitchell! As a valued reader, you get access to a **special bonus ebook** to help you get even more out of Windows 11.

⬇ **To download your free ebook, simply scan the QR code.**

Enjoy your reading and have fun with Windows 11!

If you have any trouble accessing your bonus, don't worry! You can contact the author through : ☞ https://www.facebook.com/share/1AJfQka46h/ ☞ bookovershubhelpdesk@gmail.com

Enjoy your reading and have fun with Windows 11!

Tony

www.ingramcontent.com/pod-product-compliance
Lightning Source LLC
LaVergne TN
LVHW081658050326

832903LV00026B/1808